John Robson

How a one-legged Rebel lives

Reminiscences of the civil war

John Robson

How a one-legged Rebel lives
Reminiscences of the civil war

ISBN/EAN: 9783337224578

Printed in Europe, USA, Canada, Australia, Japan

Cover: Foto ©ninafisch / pixelio.de

More available books at **www.hansebooks.com**

How A One-Legged Rebel Lives.

REMINISCENCES OF
THE CIVIL WAR.

THE STORY OF THE CAMPAIGNS OF
STONEWALL JACKSON,
AS TOLD BY A
HIGH PRIVATE IN THE "FOOT CAVALRY."

From Alleghany Mountain to Chancellorsville!

With the Complete Regimental Rosters of both the Great Armies at Gettysburg.

Concluding with a trip from Catlettsburg to Pike, Ky.

By JOHN S. ROBSON,
LATE OF THE 52D REGIMENT VIRGINIA INFANTRY.

CHRONICLE STEAM PRINTING CO., CHARLOTTESVILLE, VA., 1891

To the Reader—Greeting:

MY CHIEF OBJECT in this work is to get something to support myself with—in fact, it is a scheme founded on food, raiment and shelter, which I find hard to come at by one in my situation, there being so few positions open to a man maimed as I am, with no more education and business training than I possess; but, nevertheless, I am no applicant for charity.

I honestly believe that my little book is well worth its price, and I claim for it strict historic accuracy in all its details.

I have been materially aided in its preparation by gentlemen well posted by experience and reading in the history of the war, and not one-half of the collected data has been used, because space could not be afforded, but I hope to follow this by another, if this candidate for public favor should be successful, and my experience in the past with the big-hearted, generous people of this country—North and South—justifies my promise to finish the work now begun, and add some pages to the history of the "Cruel War" which would otherwise be forgotten.

How A One-Legged Rebel Lives!

CHAPTER I.

In fulfilling the promise of my title page, I must begin at the beginning, and tell how I came to be a "one-legged" rebel, which interesting result was brought about by the skill and enterprise of certain surgeons of the C. S. A., who amputated the other leg; but it goes without telling that the reason I was a rebel, "so-called," was my Old Virginia birth, which occurred in Rappahannock county on the 26th of March, 1844.

I do not contemplate autobiography, nor very much of general history, and if, in putting my story together, I should fail to round my periods handsomely and omit the high-toned and classic allusions to Achilles and Hector, the Trojan Horse and Ulysses, Richard and Saladin, these, more or less, of the boys who figured in ages past, and which should adorn my pages, I hope my lenient reader will travel the road far enough with me to learn that I am, unfortunately, lacking in classic lore, and cannot compare in erudition with a "Mosby," a Gen. "Dick" Taylor or a John Esten Cooke, who would fight you a battle, gloriously, to-day with the sword, and fight it over again for you to-morrow as gracefully with the pen. I was "nothing but a private," and a very junior one at that, when the late disturbance between the top and bottom of the map of the United States occurred, but

I took a very lively interest in the arbitration from its very commencement.

At that time I was a sixteen-year-old, under instruction at Mossy Creek Academy, in Augusta county—just the right age to have a good deal of fool in my composition, and at exactly the right place to develop that quality, for if there was any one point more than another, in all Virginia, where the war fever struck hard, as an epidemic, it was in Augusta county; and it required long time and strong medicine, too, to cure it up there in the valley; but it *was* cured, and now we no more wish or expect to see the armed legions of sectional hate wheeling and clanking through blood and desolation in the beautiful Valley of Virginia.

On the 16th June, 1861, my patriotism boiled over, and I volunteered under Capt. James Huddell, in Company D, 52d Regiment Virginia Infantry, commanded then by that noble Virginia gentleman, statesman and soldier, Col. John B. Baldwin, of Staunton, and we remained near that place until the 10th September; being licked into soldier shape by dint of discipline, drill, and duty, when we marched, by way of Buffalo Gap, to Crab Bottom, in Highland county, at the head of Jackson's river.

At this place stands a barn, the property of Jacob Hebner, from the eaves of which the water flows north and south—one way into the Potomac and the other into the James, the head-springs of the two rivers being here only a stone's-throw apart; and, like the sentiment of the country at that time, taking the widest divergent direction to be brought together again, after measuring their full course, in one common destiny at the ocean.

It is interesting, sometimes, to the old veterans, to go back, in retrospect, to the days of '61, when soldier-life was gilded with the glory that was to be, and we were making our first preparations for the field in a war which we were taught to think would be a very short one—ninety days at most, but which tried our faith, nerve and patience, for four of the longest years that are ever crowded into the lifetime of one generation. And believing that some account of what we did and how we managed at that time, will be of interest to the general reader, and especially to the children of the old soldiers, I have ventured to draw on the treasury of memory, and the interesting little book of my friend, Carlton McCarthy, for what is fast fading away. We who passed through it can smile now at our crude ideas of what was then necessary to make up the outfit for war of the infantry soldier, but it won't be long until we shall all have passed "over the river," and the memory of those little things which made the Confederate soldier what he was, will die too; and though the historians will tell, with eloquent pen, of the grand movements of armies and of the deeds of the Generals, he will hardly stop to explain how the private soldier was evolved from the farmer, the clerk, the mechanic, the school-boy, and transformed into the perfect, all-enduring, untiring and invincible soldier, who broiled his bacon on a stick and baked his bread on a ramrod.

The volunteer of '61 was a very elaborate institution, and entertained the idea that he was little, if any inferior to Napoleon, in his capacity and possibilities, and he of the South was very sure that he was a match, in the field, for any five Yankees in the United

States; an idea which was, to a certain extent, eliminated along with other erroneous ones which, at the outbreak of the disturbance, were entertained.

In his preparation for the campaign the Confederate soldier was forced to depend upon home resources, and in the first place he thought big boots, the higher the better, were essential to his military appearance; but he learned after awhile that a broad bottomed shoe was very much lighter to carry and easier on his ankles.

He also thought he must wear a very heavy padded coat, with long tails and many buttons, but this too proved an error, and a very short experience induced him to lay aside the coat and substitute a short-waisted, single-breasted jacket, which transformation gave the "Rebs" the universal title of "Gray Jackets" by the neighbors over the way—the Yankees.

We went in heavy on fancy caps, wavelocks and other cockady and stately head-gear, but these early gave way to the comfortable slouch hat, and to this day the Confederate veterans are much mystified when they read of the French and Prussians wearing the little caps and heavy helmets on the march and in the field, but the volunteer of '61 was a fearfully and wonderfully gotten up representative of the Sons of Mars in the first flush of his war-fever. He carried more baggage then than a major-general did afterwards, and many of these "high privates" were followed by their own faithful body-servants, who did their cooking, washing and foraging, blacked those imposing boots, dusted his clothes, and bragged to the other negroes of what a noble soldier and gentleman "Massa Tom" or "Massa Dick" was.

The knapsack was a terror, loaded with thirty to fifty pounds of surplus baggage, consisting of all manner of extra underwear, towels, combs, brushes, blacking, looking-glasses, needles, thread, buttons, bandages, everything thought of as necessary, and strapped on the outside were two great, heavy blankets and a gun or oilcloth. His haversack, too, hung on his shoulder, and always had a good stock of provisions, as though a march across the Sahara might at any time be imminent. The inevitable canteen, with contents more or less, was also slung from the shoulder, and most of the boys thought a bold soldier's outfit for the war was absolutely incomplete unless he was supplied with long gloves. In fact, the volunteer of '61 made himself a complete beast of burden, and was so heavily clad, weighted and cramped that a march was absolute torture, and the wagon trains of mess-chests and camp equipage were so immense in proportion to the number of men that it would have been impossible to guard them in an enemy's country, or anywhere else, against enterprising cavalry. However, wisdom is born of experience, and before many campaigns has been worried through the private soldier, reduced to the minimum, consisted of one man, one hat, one jacket, one pair pants, one pair drawers, one pair socks, one pair shoes, and his baggage was one blanket, one gum-cloth and one haversack, while the wonderfully-constructed mess-chests, with lids convertible into cozy dining tables, and with numerous divisions and subdivisions in nooks and cases for the holding of all imaginable necessaries and luxuries, of tea and coffee, spices and condiments, dishes, cups, vases and spoons, were *stored* nevermore to see the light in the army again, and the company property consisted of two or three skillets and frying-pans, which didn't take up much wagon room—for the infantryman generally preferred to stick the handle of the mess frying-pan into the barrel of a musket and thus be sure of having it at a given point on the march when the minimum weight soldier got there, for the wagon got to be very unreliable for the transportation of anything but ammunition; but sometimes they carried a small quantity of commissary stores, generally for the use of the train quartermaster and his staff.

The most important *appearing* personage in the army was the aforesaid quartermaster, who always managed to have saved for his own use, out of the scanty supplies, an abundance of the best, and as all drivers and assistants in his department held their "bomb-proofs" at his supreme pleasure, he had it in his power at all times to control freights. His handsome, flashy, lace-trimmed uniform of fine gray cloth, adorned with the star or bar of his rank, caused the folks along the line of march to imagine they had the pivilege of gazing at some of the famous generals—Longstreet, Hill, Pickett, or perhaps Lee himself—when in fact the generals, in their dingy dress, had passed unnoticed, and this gaily caparisoned cavalier was only a quartermaster marshaling a little wagon train in rear of the army.

The Confederate soldier held on to his haversack, not to carry food in as is popularly supposed, but it was the ever present receptacle for tobacco, pipes, strings, buttons and the like, and very often when, with great display and bluster by the commissaries, three days' rations were issued to the men, they would cook and eat the whole lot at one meal, which was decidedly the most convenient way of carrying it, and besides it was usually the case that they had been without food for from two to five meals, and it was not much of an exploit to consume the small quantity issued for what was termed "three days' rations," and after eating it, they would trust to luck and strategy for meals, or go hungry, as usual, till the next ration day.

The commissary department of the Southern Confederacy was most scandalously mismanaged from the beginning, and the commissary general, Colonel Northrop, was the worst and most complete failure, North or South, of the whole war, in consequence of which the men were forced to forage for themselves. As the war progressed and this stern "mother of invention" and "neutralizer of all law," Necessity, and Hunger, her child, made themselves felt in all their force, it was no uncommon sight to see a whole brigade marching in solid column along a road one minute and the next scattered over a big brier field picking the blackberries, but as soon as the gleaning was done all would return to the ranks and resume the march as though nothing had happened to break it, and in the fall of the year a persimmon tree would halt a column as long as a 'simmon was on it.

We had no sutlers in our army; the blockade and dearth of marketable funds prevented that, the nearest approach to it being the occasional old darkey with his cider cart or basket of pies and cakes—so called—and it was almost marvelous to see how quick the old contraband's stock would be cleaned out.

The rebel soldier depended much upon the supplies he could get from the enemy in battle, for the Yankees were always abundantly supplied, and thus we had a double incentive to win the fight.

A federal officer who was conversing with Gen. Jackson in the street of Harper's Ferry, at its surrender in Sept., '62, says that an orderly galloped up to "Stonewall" and said: "General, I am ordered by Gen. McLaws to report to you that McClellan's whole army is within six miles, and coming this way." Jackson took no notice of it at all, and the orderly turned to ride back when the General called to him, "has Gen. McClellan a drove of cattle or a wagon train with him?" The orderly replied that he had. "All right," said Jackson, "I can whip any army that is followed by a drove of cattle;" alluding to the hungry condition of his men, and the good fighting qualities thereby developed when beef was in sight.

Stealing is a low vice, no matter who does it, but that hungry men should take whatever they found in the eating line is not to be wondered at, and the old Irish adage, "There's no law for a hungry man," should be borne in mind when judging the soldier.

In the early days, when the volunteers were being mustered for "twelve months, unless sooner discharged," and the idea of a short war was being industriously promulgated by the big men of the cross roads, and the newspaper generals at the county seats, the boys were very uneasy about it, for fear it would wind up before they could get in.

When the first Manassas was fought, the 52nd Va. was sorely disgruntled, believing they had been left out for a purpose, and jealousy rankled hot in our hearts at sight of the battery boys, and others, from Staunton, who were sporting around town with bullet-wounds and bloody bandages, the idols of the girls and made heroes of by everybody. Fate was against us, for we had not even seen the smoke of that first great battle from afar, and we would have resigned a kingdom without a murmur to have had one of those wounds; even a very small wound would have been thankfully received, and we noticed also that the accounts and descriptions of the battle were considered much more accurate and authentic when related by some fellow with his arm in a sling and a general air about him of—"stand aside! I am holier than thou," "been wounded at Manassas;" although it might be that he got crippled under a wagon, and never saw a Yankee.

But every one of these veteran heroes of that battle was supposed to have slain at least four Yankees, and fought Sherman's battery with bowie knife. "Charging" the batteries of the enemy was the favorite amusement of the lucky fellows who were at Manassas, and every one of them had "charged," more or less, batteries that day, and the men who captured the "long Tom" rifle piece were wonderfully numerous.

CHAPTER II.

I must now return to the camp at Crab Bottom, because our stay was brief, and the rumors of the operations of our great Generals in the mountains were numerous. There was always news, and Floyd, Wise, Loring, Lee, Johnston, and other great commanders of the Confederacy, were measuring lances with Milroy, Rosecrans, McClellan, Cox, Tyler, Schenck, &c, of the Federal Army, for the control of the empire of Western Virginia, and the time has come, in my story, for the 52nd to "mix in," as Forrest, the famous cavalryman, would say.

We marched towards Moorefield, but stopped at a camp called "Straight Creek," in Highland county, and were joined by Capt. Shumaker, with his battery from "Camp Bartow," and here we did have a most glorious time of it, in the perfect autumn weather of the mountain glades and vales, and oh! such living! The memory of the buckwheat and honey, the cakes, pies, roast beef and wild turkey, lingers lingeringly, and I would I were a boy again in camp with the old 52nd; but the regiment has made its last march on this side the shadow land, and nothing is left but the glorious memory of the good time gone.

While here an incident occurred which made quite an impression on my boyish mind, and I very much doubt if it has been forgotten by the oldest survivor. Our camp was on the bank of a creek and just below the point where a mill dam was located. It was quite a large dam and had been sufficient, up to this time, to hold the accumulated water in check, but now it chose to give way, and sweeping like a mighty flood through the camp it overwhelmed tents, barracks, bunks, and all pertaining to our little military, in one universal ruin. We were completely washed out, and the disaster served, in a measure, to reconcile us to the movement we were soon called to make to Alleghany mountain; and now our soldier life began to lose gilding.

Our regiment was ordered to report to Gen. H. R. Jackson, of Georgia, a veteran of the Mexican war, in which he was a Colonel of Volunteers, who had been left with two brigades, by Gen. Lee, to hold the crossing at Greenbrier river of the turnpike leading from Staunton to Parkersburg across Cheat mountain, and after passing through the intervening valley, and then the Alleghany mountain into our own Valley.

Jackson's camp here was called "Camp Bartow," from one of the heroes of Manassas, the lamented Colonel of the 8th Georgia.

The Southern camp was on the south bank of the river, here not more than twenty yards wide, but Col. Baldwin had, by order of Gen. Jackson, posted our regiment at the Alleghany pass, in our rear. When the Federals learned of the withdrawal of the large body of Southern troops towards the Kanawha, they determined to move the balance of us, and Gen. Reynolds, of brilliant Gettysburg fame, organized a force of 6,000 troops, with twelve pieces of artillery, and moving from their camp, on the summit of Cheat mountain, on the 2nd Oct., came down on Camp Bartow with great gallantry; but Jackson's two little brigades, commanded by Col.'s Johnson and Taliaferro, stood their ground so stubbornly that, after exhausting all their means to drive them from the field, in a battle commencing early on Thursday morning, Oct. 3, and continuing till half-past two o'clock P. M., the Federals retreated in confusion, losing over 300 men killed and wounded, while Jackson's loss was 6 killed, 31 wounded and 12 missing.

Gen. Reynolds had intended to clear the turnpike, and march to Staunton, but not succeeding in getting

"Camp Bartow," he failed to approach our post at Alleghany pass and, to our chagrin, we had lost another opportunity to fight the Yankees, so we grumbled savagely—fully satisfied now that the war would end and we would not have any show at all to distinguish ourselves. However, we "roughed it," soldier fashion, and grew very familiar with the mountains; in fact, we might have been mistaken, from our language, for a corps of topographical engineers, so extensively did we talk of what was being done in our department. Go where you would about the camp, such geographical remarks as "Gen. Lee is moving on the Yanks at Elkwater," "Gen. Floyd is going to cut them off at Meadow Bluffs," "Old Gov. Wise will knock 'em out at Sewell mountain," "Rosecrans whipped at Lewisburg;" "we will flank them by way of Carnifax Ferry;" and we used to bet largely on what "Ned." Johnson would do when Taliaferro's brigade joined him. We had an idea that a regiment of Southern troops was something fearful to run against, and as for a brigade—well, it was simply irresistible—in fact every man was a general, and knew exactly what to do next, no matter what had been the result of the last movement. But discouraging days were at hand, and when winter come upon us great numbers of the men got sick, and the mountain fogs and frosts were harder to contend with than the enemy.

When Gen. Floyd made his march from the Gauley river to Fayette C. H., he had to transport more than 800 sick men, and although he was for twenty days engaged in skirmishing and fighting the Yankees for the right of way, his killed and wounded only amounted to 14. After the fight at Greenbrier river, Gen. H. R. Jackson was sent on duty to Georgia; Taliaferro's brigade was withdrawn towards Staunton; Camp Bartow was only occupied by scouts and pickets, and our line of defence was drawn back to Alleghany mountain, fourteen miles from Greenbrier river and the same distance from Montery, with Col. Edward Johnson in command, with about 1,200 men, consisting of the 12th Georgia, 31st Virginia, the 52nd Virginia, under Col. Baldwin, the battalions of Hansborough and Riger, and two batteries of four 6-pounders under Captains Anderson and Miller, also one company of cavalry under Col. Flournoy, and here, with a scanty supply of blankets and rations, in the keen, frosty air of the mountains we actually suffered.

About this time a name, afterwards well-known in the Valley, was much talked of, and on the 13th of Dec., its owner, Gen. R. H. Milroy, appeared in our front, with a force which, his own people said, amounted to 8,000.

His first move on our line was made at Slavin's Crossing, about three miles from Camp Bartow on the 18th, where Major Ross, with the volunteers of the brigade, with 100 men, met the advance of the enemy and checked their movement long enough for Col. Johnson to get ready for them; and the next morning the *great* General Milroy's army came up hunting a fight, and I am of the opinion to this day that nobody had to waste time hunting a fight around old Ed. Johnson without getting as much as was good for them before night.

The Virginians and Georgians had a hot breakfast

all ready for Milroy's folks as soon as they got there, and the 31st Virginia, especially, was very hospitable in their reception. This regiment was mostly composed of N. W. Va. men, and Milroy stood between them and home, which appeared to make them particularly severe on him, and their gallant commander, Major Boykin, led them with dauntless spirit. I had a splendid position in this battle and could see the whole fight without having to take any part in it, and I remember how I thought Col. Johnson must be the most wonderful hero in the world, as I saw him at one point, where his men were hard pressed, snatch a musket in one hand and swinging a big club in the other he led his line right up among the enemy, driving them headlong down the mountain, killing and and wounding many with the bayonet and capturing a large number of prisoners; but the "boys in blue" fought stubbornly, and many of our men were killed here on the left of the road. On the right, the enemy, in strong force, posted in a mountain clearing, among the fallen timber, stumps, and brush, was too much for the Rebs, until the veteran, Capt. Anderson, brought his battery into position and thundered a storm of round shot and canister among them, knocking their timber defences about their heads, and making their nest too hot to hold them; and they too, retreated to Cheat Mountain, but for quite awhile they were pelted by Anderson's guns and by Miller's battery, which got in in the nick of time.

Capt. Anderson was killed just as the Yankees were breaking up into the retreat by a party he mistook for some of our own infantry lying between his guns and the enemy, and riding forward he called them to come back into the line, at the same time beckoning to them with his head, when they fired a full volley at him, which killed him instantly. He had been through three wars, and had taken part in fifty-eight pitched battles.

Lieutenant Raines, of Lynchburg, took command of Anderson's battery, and the other battery, under Capt. Miller, had been originally mustered into the 52d, but was taken out and organized as artillery during the preceding summer.

My recollections of Col. Edward Johnson, as he appeared that day, is very distinct, partly, perhaps, because it was the first real battle I had ever witnessed, but mainly, I think, because he acted so differently from all my preconceived ideas of how a commander should act on the field of battle. He was a native of Chesterfield county, Virginia, but at the opening of the war was living in Georgia, and came from there at the first outbreak of hostile preparations in command of the 12th Georgia regiment. After this battle he was made brigadier, and in February, '63, was promoted to major-general, and commanded a division in Ewell's corps, composed of the brigades of Walker, Stewart and J. M. Jones.

He was noted all through the war as a stubborn fighter, and was known throughout the country after this victory as " Alleghany " Johnson.

In the battle of Alleghany Mountain the Federals admitted a loss of four hundred killed and wounded, while ours, by actual returns, was twenty-five killed and ninety-seven wounded—not more than skirmishing afterwards, but we rated it as a big battle then.

The next day I was on detail with the burial party,

and while putting away two dead Yankees who had been in the party that killed Capt. Anderson, we found in their pockets the first greenbacks I had ever seen. We considered the bills curiosities in the way of currency and only valued them as such, not believing that such money would be of any more value than the continental currency was after the Revolution, for of course the North was to be defeated and impoverished by the war, and not able to redeem her promise to pay. In fact, at that time, we would not have given ten cents on the dollar for it in Confederate money, which goes to sustain the statement elsewhere made that I, as a type of the volunteer of '61, had a considerable touch of *fool* in my composition, because any person of common sense must have known that the war money of an already established government must, of necessity, have a better show for value than that of an experiment, no matter who might be the final winner in the contest, but the faith that was in us was strong indeed.

After the battle of Alleghany Mountain some half-dozen of our Company died; in fact, nearly all the wounded died from cold and exposure to the inclement winter weather, and we all suffered severely. We soon moved our camp to Shenandoah Mountain, where Gen. Johnson left us for a while to attend to important business in Richmond, and Col. Baldwin commanded the department, and we remained here until the general movement of armies took place in March, 1862. We made our winter quarters as comfortable as we knew how, but we were green campaigners, and the best we knew was awkward enough. We had got some tents, and these with log huts and plenty of fire kept us in some sort of comfort, but during this bleak winter the boys talked a good deal about their "twelve month's" term of enlistment expiring in the spring, and not quite so much of their fear that the war would be too short to give them a taste. Our next movement was to the old camp at West View, six miles from Staunton, and in preparing for this we burned up completely our camp at Shenandoah Mountain, tents and all, which puzzled exceedingly the generals of the rank and file, and it has always remained a mystery to me why we did it, for there was no enemy in threatening distance so far as we knew.

While waiting for developments, "us generals" were passing through an ordeal of electioneering, because the term of service for nearly the whole army had expired and the time for reorganization of companies and regiments had arrived, and enlistments "for the period of the war."

To offer a man promotion in the early period of the war was almost an insult, and the higher the social position, the greater the wealth, the more patriotic it would be to serve in the humble position of private in the ranks; and I have seen many men of education and ability refusing promotion, and carrying their muskets under command of officers greatly their inferiors, mentally and morally, as soldiers. It was not uncommon to see ex-congressmen and judges, as well as preachers, tramping along in ranks as privates, but one year of soldiering had engendered a desire for commissions in the hearts of many, and, in some cases, much trickery was resorted to by aspirants to secure the soldier vote for company offices.

Our regiment, at reorganization, had been changed somewhat, Col. Baldwin having been retired to a seat in the Confederate States Congress.

Col. M. G. Harman commanded, with Lieut.-Col. J. H. Skinner and Major Ross as field officers, and Lieut. Lewis, from the Institute (V. M. I.), was Adjutant; Company A was commanded by Capt. Garber; Company B by Capt. Long; Company C by Capt. Dabney; Company D by Capt. Ayrehart; Company E by Capt. Wadkins; Company F by Capt. Cline; Company G by Capt. Bateman; Company H by Capt. Lilly; Company I by Capt. Humphreys; and Company K by Capt. Walton.

I could not give the roll of each company in the 52nd if I would—but I would if I could: for I think it ought to be preserved, and I hope the names of the gallant boys will yet be saved.

CHAPTER III.

Every story should have its hero, and as I have no idea myself of posing as such, I can't think it at all improper to make, for my central figure in this part of my little book which treats of the war, the immortal "Stonewall" Jackson, whose fortunes as a commander I am proud to have followed from the day of McDowell to that of his death. We had not heard much of him, apart from the record he made at Manassas, until reports of his *crazy* battle at Kernstown, as it was called, were received; and although it was the custom in that war for both sides to magtify their victories and depreciate their defeats, we were pretty strongly impressed with the belief that Jackson had been pretty badly worsted at Kernstown, by that fighting Irishman, Gen. Shields, whom we rated always as a gentleman and a soldier ; and when we learned that Jackson was retreating up the Valley before Banks, our faith was visibly weakened, for we knew Milroy was pushing towards our own position with a much larger force than we could muster.

Our accounts from Jackson were not all painted in black, for we learned that he had matched his four thousand "foot cavalry" against Shields' ten thousand, and had fought so fierce and fast that the high-blooded Irishman thought Jackson had two thousand the most men, and we trusted largely in his skill ; and were not totally dissatisfied when he turned up at West View, as though to cut out some work for "Alleghany" Johnson's men, which, of course, we thought unnecessary, all of us being *generals*, and able to lay our plans without his supervision, but he seems to have been arranging matters to suit Gen. Banks, who, about this time, telegraphed McClellan that he "had forced the Rebel, Jackson, to permanently abandon the Valley and retreat on Gordonsville in eastern Virginia."

This is a verbatim report of Banks' message, and shows that he knew very little about Mr. Jackson, and it also shows that Jackson had succeeded—so far as the Federal Generals knew—in getting completely lost, a thing he took a great deal of interest in doing repeatedly, during the progress of the war ; but Gen. Milroy, marching from the west towards Staunton for the express purpose of crushing Johnson, found Jackson at McDowell, in Highland county, with his chaplain, Dr. Dabney, holding worship in his camp.

On May 7th, '62, Gen. Johnson, with his six regiments, was ready for the fray, and Jackson's Valley division, formed of the brigades of Taliaferro, Winder and Campbell, with the Lexington Cadets under Gen. F. H. Smith, of the Institute, were on hand to back us up with aid and comfort.

Gen. Johnson, who knew the country almost as well as if he had made it, led the advance and drove four regiments of the enemy from Shenandoah mountain, capturing their camps, with tents, clothes, arms and commissary stores, and placed his men in bivouac on the camp ground of the enemy. He had already formed his forces into two brigades commanded by Cols. Scott and Connor, our boys being under Col. Scott, who had the 44th, 52nd and 58th Virginia.

The 52nd took position on Sutlington Hill. When the enemy advanced to the attack we received the full assault of their first line and repulsed it, thus giving time for the arrival of the other regiments. The enemy, after being driven back, opened on us with their artillery a rapid and incessant fire of case shot and shell, but "us boys" laid low among the rocks and trees which afforded us ample protection, and also the angle of elevation of their guns being so great, no damage, except to the timber, resulted from this cannonade, and the noise was all on the Yankees' side, we having no artillery in position.

About 5 o'clock, Gen. Milroy, having been joined by Gen. Schenck, advanced his whole force of 8,000 men, and the battle roared and raged along the side of the hill with terrific force, for a long time, but our two little brigades held them back until Jackson got his flank movement worked out, and then the Federals gave way, as a matter of course. In the final closing up of the business, just as Taliaferro's brigade reached the field, the 52nd, backed up by the 10th Va., made a charge which drove them headlong down the hill and the battle ended at 8 o'clock p. m. It seemed to me we had been at it about a week, but the other boys spoke as though it was a very short half a day.

The fight had been hotly contested, but Milroy made it perfectly clear to all on both sides that he was no match for Jackson in handling troops in battle, notwithstanding his superiority in numbers.

Our loss was 71 killed and 390 wounded, but we could not learn that of the enemy, as they still held their main camp and carried away their dead and wounded during the battle, with their well served ambulance corps, but we found 103 dead on the mountain side next morning; and during the night Milroy set the woods on fire behind him, and retreated towards Franklin, whither Gen. Jackson followed the next day.

On the 14th of May, about 3 miles from the town, he drew up his little army in a small valley and spoke a few words of commendation of their gallantry at McDowell, in his short, curt tone, and appointed 10 o'clock that day as an occasion of prayer and thanksgiving for the victory—which was duly observed—notwithstanding the firing of Milroy's cannon-balls over our heads, but many of us, during the exercises, prayed with real devotion, by the book, "from battle, murder, and sudden death, good Lord deliver us."

Gen. Jackson stood motionless, with bent, bare head, and as soon as the meeting was over, marched his army back to McDowell, and the next day crossed the Shenandoah mountain, halting at Lebanon Springs, where he gave his men some much needed rest, and an opportunity to observe the day appointed by the President for fasting and prayer.

But I must repeat that I am not attempting a history of the war, only trying to follow in a weak, one-legged, halting manner, the boys of the 52nd, in doing which I must call to mind the pleasant bivouac in the lovely Mossy Creek valley, with headquarters at Major M. G. McCue's house, and where all the people were so hospitable and kind to the jaded Rebels, and from whence we moved to Mt. Zion Church, near Mt. Solon, and I had the pleasure of a day at my uncle's, Dr. Geo. T. Robson, which place I had left one year before, a gay, young volunteer marching to the war and very much afraid I was too late to get any fighting; but I confess I was not now so very much *afraid* of missing a battle as I had been, and I think that year had taken some of the conceit out of me.

However, we could not tarry long in our pleasant quarters, for "Stonewall" was restless, and the Federal Generals—Banks, Fremont, Shields, McDowell and Milroy were either in, or threatening his beloved Valley of Virginia, to surrender which, he declared, was to give up Virginia; and in this campaign we soon found that events were hurrying fast, and we must do likewise or get left; which recalls to mind a true story of Col. William Smith, of the 49th Virginia, universally known as "Extra Billy:"

On one occasion he was endeavoring to get his men in marching order as quick as possible, but they were very dilatory about it, and paid so little attention to his oft-repeated command to "fall in here, men, fall in I say!" as to excite the Colonel's ire, whereupon he testily exclaimed, "If you don't fall in here right away now, I'll march the regiment off and leave every d—— one of you behind!"

Our "Stonewall" was no such Irishman as that, for when he marched his army off he was pretty sure to take it all along, and at this time, with all the odds the fortune of war had arrayed against him, he surely needed every man. It is, perhaps, not out of place here to attempt a description of the impression "Stonewall" Jackson made upon me and my comrades who had never seen him, until he got lost from Mr. Banks and turned up at Valley Mills near McDowell. I shall not attempt any description of his person or appearance, for that has been done so often that everybody who reads Southern history at all know all about it, but on first view I thought it hardly possible that he could be much of a general, and if the vernacular of to-day had been in vogue then, I think I should have reported that I had seen a "crank," and I believe most of the men of the 52d would have pronounced the opinion correct; but my reader must remember that most of us were still generals ourselves to some extent, though we did not consider our generalship quite so infallible as we formerly thought, and the killing and wounding of our comrades at Alleghany and McDowell had opened our eyes wonderfully to the probabilities of what might eventually grow out of this war if something or somebody didn't stop it. Colonel M. G. Harman (Col. of 52d Va.) was wounded severely in the arm; John Harman was killed and his brother George wounded; Stoutemoy and many others, and Lieut. John Carson, of Company D, (the Co. to which I belonged) a gallant soldier and Christian gentleman, had been killed. But memory fails me now, and I cannot record, as my heart prompts me to do, the names of the gallant boys who fought and fell for the cause they loved so well and thought was right.

When the thought of our noble dead rolls over my heart, I love to read the lines of Father Ryan, and get comfort from the sentiments so beautifully expressed by our charming soldier-poet:

>'Tis o'er, the fearful struggle o'er,
>   The bloody contest past,
> And hearts oppressed with anxious care
>   Throb peacefully at last.
> Those who were spared are with us now,
>   Some are in Heaven, we trust;
> But though the victory is not ours,
>   They're glorious in the dust.
>
> How many fell whose names and deeds
>   Are unrecorded here,
> Save in some lonely, widowed heart,
>   Or by the orphan's tear!
> Yet these were they who swelled the ranks
>   Of our brave Southern host,
> And though no stone now marks their graves,
>   They're glorious in the dust.
>
> Long shall we mourn for those whose lives
>   Were offered up in vain;
> We miss them in our vacant homes,
>   Nor can from tears refrain.
> Forever cherished in our hearts,
>   Their names nor deeds can rust,
> And tho' they sleep beneath the sod,
>   They're glorious in the dust.

And there are names we may not speak,
  But yet to all how dear,
For them our daily prayers ascend,
  May God, in mercy, hear.
How have they suffered, maimed for life!
  Their highest hopes, how crushed;
But with a manly spirit borne,
  They're glorious in the dust.

Bravely we fought and bravely fell,
  Nor gained the victor crown,
Still we will prove that Southern hearts
  Can suffer and be strong—
Strong in affection, honor, truth,
  Strong in the Christian's trust;
'Tis trial brightens faith and hope,
  We're glorious in the dust.

If in my power, the names of those who fought and fell for the "Lost Cause," should be graven in golden letters on a granite monument, to endure as time: as a tribute to pure patriotism and unselfish devotion to home and native land, in withstanding for all those bloody years the assaults of myriads of all nations and tongues, marshalled for the desolation of our loved Southern land and the subjugation of our people.

The principles for which the Confederate soldier fought and died, are today the harmony of this country, and so long as those principles were held in abeyance the country was in turmoil and almost ruin.

The heart is greater than the mind, and it is not fair to demand reasons for actions which are above reason, and the people of the South, refusing to receive the dogmas of fanaticism as gospel, and to submit to the tyranny of fanatics, they became Rebels. Being such they must be punished, and for resistance they died; but their soldier boys died with their "boots on," and smoking guns in their hands. And they fought all the odds of overwhelming numbers, thoroughly armed and equipped with all the latest inventions of warfare; fought all the host of ills, which came from blockaded ports, empty treasury vaults, the wails of distress from home, cold, hunger, nakedness; fought, *without* pay, the legions of the Northern army, who had regular monthly pay, in good money, with big bounties, plenty to eat, and abundance of clothing, blankets and tents, and superb hospital outfits, with all that sanitary commission could suggest for the comfort of sick and wounded; while the Confederate soldier could get no medicine when sick; nor, often, when amputation was necessary, even chloroform to numb the agony caused by the knife and saw of the surgeon. The Confederate soldier fought against the commerce of the United States, and all the facilities for war which Europe could supply, and laid down life for life with hireling hosts of Germans, Irish, Italians, English, French, Chinese, Japanese, white, black and brown.

CHAPTER IV.

I had almost forgotten that we are on the march with "Stonewall" Jackson down the Valley, and we want to keep up, for although the complicated movements of McClellan on the Peninsula, McDowell in front of Washington, Banks in the Valley, Shields along the Blue Ridge, and Fremont and Milroy in the mountains of Western Virginia, were enough to puzzle the brain of the most thorough master of the art of war in any age, they do not appear to have disquieted or embarrassed Jackson in the least. He looked right through the cloud of mystery to the plain object to be attained, viz., the diversion of re-enforcements from McClellan's "grand army," and he went at the accomplishment of this purpose with the mathematical accuracy and resistless force of a Corliss engine in motion. Past Harrisonburg we tramped rapidly, and by the 20th had reached New Market, on the Valley pike, where the road to Luray across the Massanutton—the glory of the Valley—leads into the Page valley, and here, for the first time, we up-country boys saw General Ashby, whose fame as a cavalry leader had reached us so brilliantly, and thenceforward the troopers of Ashby hung as an impenetrable veil in front and flank, so perfectly screening our movements that Gen. Banks never knew where to look for his tormentor—Jackson—and it is doubtful if he yet knew whether or not this "rebel" was still at Gordonsville, in eastern Virginia.

We took the right-hand road at New Market, and at night united with Gen. Ewell's division, which had come down the river from Swift Run Gap.

On the afternoon of the next day—23d May, 1862, when we had passed Luray a long distance—a funny incident occurred, which, perhaps, Gen. Jackson may have been expecting. The column was marching along at a swinging gait—getting over ground pretty lively—when a young and rather good-looking woman rushed out of the woods, so agitated and out of breath that she could scarcely speak, but coming up to the General, who had turned to meet her, she soon began to talk with great volubility. We, of course, could not hear what she was saying, nor could we even conjecture the import of her mission, but it was subsequently made known that this was the famous woman spy and scout, Belle Boyd, and the information she detailed right there to Gen. Jackson with the precision of a staff officer, was to the effect that Front Royal was just beyond the woods, a short distance ahead; that the town was full of Federal troops; that their camp was on the west side of the river, where they had cannon in position to cover the wagon bridge, but none to protect the railroad bridge below; that the Yankees believed Jackson's army was west of the Massanutton near Harrisonburg, and knew nothing of the movement of Ewell's division; that Banks had moved his headquarters to Winchester, twenty miles northwest of Front Royal, and was looking for the Rebels to advance by the Valley pike, and when they did he intended to strike their flank and rear with his Front Royal detachment, all of which was absolutely true, but it was known to Gen. Jackson the night we left New Market and only needed Belle Boyd to confirm it; and when the "foot cavalry" got knowledge of this matter, as they did in few days, their opinion of their leader changed, and blind, awkward and queer as he *seemed* they knew he was anything but a crank.

The movement to Front Royal was nearly to a focus now, and Gen. "Dick" Taylor started his Louisiana brigrade — a "daisy" she was, too — at a double, closely followed by the whole force, and pretty soon we broke cover down a steep by-path into the Gooney Manor road, not half a mile from town.

Some cavalry was first encountered, but almost instantly brushed away, and our cavalry, making a sweep, captured and brought out many prisoners.

The Louisianians, led by the gallant General, went at the railroad bridge, and then came Col. Bradley T. Johnson, with his regiment, the 1st Maryland, in a fair, square attack straight into Col. Kenly's 1st Maryland, of Banks' army, when "Greek literally met Greek," and the tug of war was desperate. Generals Jackson and Ewell galloped along the field, like knights of the olden time, cheering on their men; the "Tigers," of Major Wheat, and the Louisiana boys "waded in" yelling, firing, fighting; while the Virginians joined in the chorus, the 52nd well up and doing her duty equal to any on the field, and no man, woman or child, all the way from Luray, knew we were coming until we had passed, except Belle Boyd.

I wish I could give a description of the battle of Front Royal, with all the preceding incidents and operations, showing the inspiration by which Gen. Jackson planned and brought through to complete success his audacious movement right into the camps of the enemy which surrounded him, and I have always believed it was a piece of one of the sublimest pictures of strategy ever performed in war.

The enemy was pretty soon driven across the river, and tried hard to destroy the bridge, but the pressure in the rear was too great to give them time, and moreover Ashby, with part of his cavalry, had crossed above, cut the railroad and telegraph wires to Strasburg, and prevented any help coming to the enemy from that point, while at Buckton he drove them from the strong position in the railroad cut and captured a train of cars. Other portions of the cavalry overtook the retreating Federals at Cedarville, and some companies of the 6th Va. cavalry, led by Capt. Grimsley, of Culpeper, in two gallant charges, broke them up completely, but many good men of the cavalry were killed—among them Capt. Baxter, Co. K. 6th Va., and Captains Sheets and Fletcher of the Ashby Legion.

There was considerable jealousy on the part of the infantry against the cavalry, the "footpads" thinking the riders had the easiest time, and seldom omitted an opportunity to make game of them, especially when the cavalry would be passing them on a march, and the old chaff of "Come down out o' that hat, know you're thar; see your legs a hangin' down!" "Git from behin' them boots! needn't say you aint thar; see your ears a workin'!" will be remembered while any of the old soldiers live. But I think the cutest thing I ever heard was by an old infantry man, on the Valley pike, in '63. He was resting, his arms crossed on the muzzle of his musket, when a dashing-looking cavalry man, wearing considerable gold lace and feathers, rode up. The infantryman eyed him quizzically, for a few minutes, and then accosted him with, "Say, Mister, did you ever see a dead Yankee?" and paused to enjoy the contemptuously dignified, silent stare of the cavalier. The old knapsack-toter then continued: "Cause if you didn't, and you'll go along with us for about an hour we'll show you one." This failing to elicit any response, he began again, in a very reassuring tone: "You needn't not be afeered, Mister, 'cause there hain't none of our cavalry got killed yet, and I hain't never heered of but one of 'em gittin' hurt, and he was kicked while he was a currying of his creeter." Of course there was a yell, as the "wore out" cavalryman rode off as lively as he could, and the footman set his trap for the next one.

We boys didn't make so much sport of the cavalry after Front Royal, and it was no uncommon sight to see a dead man with spurs on during the Valley campaign. The artillery, too, under the famous commanders, Poague, Chew, Courtney, Carpenter, Lattimer, Caskie, Raines, Luck, Miller, Cutshaw, Wooding, and others, did splendid service.

I do not think I ever saw a list of the regiments in Jackson's army, and believing it will interest the reader will endeavor to give, from memory and reading, what I believe to be a correct statement of them:

From Virginia there were the 2d, 4th, 5th, 10th, 13th, 21st, 23d, 25th, 27th, 31st, 33d, 37th, 42d, 44th, 48th, 52d, and 58th regiments, and the 1st (Irish) battalion, infantry.

From Louisiana, the 6th, 7th, 8th and 9th regiments, and Major Wheat's "Tiger" battalion, infantry.

From Georgia, the 12th and 21st regiments, infantry.

From North Carolina, the 21st regiment, infantry.

From Alabama, the 15th regiment, infantry.

From Mississippi, the 16th regiment, infantry.

From Maryland, the 1st regiment, infantry.

The cavalry of Gen. Ashby was the 7th and 12th regiments, and the 17th battalion, Virginia, and the brigade which came over with Gen. Ewell was the 2d and 6th Virginia, with one company, under Ewell's special orders, commanded by Capt. E. V. White, from Loudoun county, Va.—making 27 regiments and

2 battalions of infantry, 4 regiments and 1 battalion of cavalry, and, I think, 11 batteries, of about 44 guns altogether.

Of course I am rambling, moving along the route towards the point where I became a "one-legged Rebel," and I got there soon enough, but it took me by Winchester on Sunday morning, May 25th, 1862, where I helped all I could to crush the life out of Gen. Banks' army, and such a glorious welcome as met us from the warm-hearted people of that famous old town. There was some fighting in the streets, but the happy inhabitants wouldn't stay indoors, not even the women and babies; but, almost frantic with delight, they with one breath blessed us for coming, and the next blamed us for letting so many Yankees get away. They evidently expected impossible things from "Stonewall's" men, such as catching crows on the wing, or the "wild gazelle on Judah's hills," either of which was as possible for us as to overtake Gen. Banks's runaways.

The singularly brilliant idea of Gen. Geo. H. Stuart, who commanded the little cavalry brigade, composed of the 2d and 6th regiments, that inasmuch as he belonged to Ewell's division he was not subject to Gen. Jackson's immediate command, permitted many of the enemy to make their escape, and the whole cavalry force was so scattered as not to be available for pursuit of the flying Federals, at the proper moment, which was unfortunate for us, but we told the Winchester folks that we had done our best, and they showed their appreciation of our efforts by standing on the streets with quantities of good things to eat, which they pressed upon the eagerly moving soldiers, and here allow me to say, from personal experience, that it was perfectly safe, under any circumstances, to force nice, roast beef, ham, biscuit, pies, cakes, pickles and the like upon any marching column of Confederate soldiers, whether they were pursuing a routed enemy or fighting him in the streets of a town, and no person who did it was ever hurt.

We had done the best we could for Mr. Banks, and were pretty well pleased with ourselves once more, so that the old spirit of "generalship" again spread its mantle over each soldier in the line, and he knew exactly how to manage the campaign thenceforward notwithstanding our ideas had not been strictly followed by Gen. Jackson in the opening of it, but we did not fully agree as to preliminaries now, some of us being strongly in favor of taking immediate march to Harrisburg, Pa., and operating from that point as a base, while many thought we should make an instant attack on Washington city itself, and thereby draw Gen. McClellan out of his intrenched lines on the Chickahominy, thereby giving Gen. Johnston the opportunity he was looking for to ruin him as we had done the armies opposed to us.

We knew we were going to hold the Valley anyhow, for of course the war was almost over now—and how we did pity the fellows at home, youngsters and the like, who wouldn't get any experience in camping, marching and fighting, nor any share of the glory that radiated around and all about "Stonewall" Jackson's men.

We had nearly made up our minds to elect "Stonewall" President of the Confederate States at the next election, although Beauregard was still the soldiers' idol, and, as yet, we had heard very little of "Marse Robert," for Seven Pines had not been fought, and "Joe Johnston," the "great retreater," was still falling back somewhere about the Peninsula. But *we* were not falling back—were not of that kind! Come to stay we had, and, like Alexander, were sedulously looking out for other armies to conquer. So it passed, and we trotted about to hurry Banks' demoralized legions over the border, and swelling with pride in *our* generalship.

While the fighting at Winchester was in progress one of the staff suggested to Gen. Jackson that he was exposing himself too much, and the answer was, "Tell the troops to push right on to the Potomac," and this became a kind of watchword with us; but Gen. Banks got there first, and promptly reported to his government that "he had accomplished a premeditated march of nearly sixty miles, in the face of the enemy, defeating his plans and giving him battle wherever found;" that he "had not suffered an attack or rout," but he naively added that "it is seldom a river-crossing of such magnitude is achieved with greater success, and there were never more grateful hearts in the same number of men than when, on the 26th, we stood on the opposite shore." These quotations are taken verbatim, by John Esten Cooke, from the records in the War Department at Washington, and if, after reading them, anybody has anything to say, I give them liberty to say it. It may be that "Stonewall" had some idea of making a "premeditated march" himself, but if so he said nothing to "us generals" about it; but we noticed that he took the unnecessary precaution—as we thought—to start Col.

Cunningham with his regiment, the 21st Va., up the pike from Winchester, as quick as he could get the stuff together, with 3,000 prisoners, 100 cattle, and a great train of wagons loaded with 34,000 pounds of bacon, with flour, salt, bread, coffee, sugar, cheese, &c., in proportion, and $125,185.00 worth of commissary stores, $25,000 worth of sutler's goods, an immense quantity of medical and hospital supplies, and 9,354 small arms, with two pieces of artillery and a great many cavalry horses and equipments. All such goods as this, though rated on the quartermaster's inventory at actual *cash* value, had been bought and paid for in another currency, more precious to many than greenbacks, gold or silver, and we go to another ledger to learn *that* price, as shown by the list of killed and wounded.

On this advance movement down the Valley every man was pressing to the front with a vim and enthusiasm which gave the enemy no rallying point or time to prepare a line of defence, and Gen. Jackson said that "the battles of Front Royal and Winchester had been fought without a straggler."

Our loss was 68 killed, 327 wounded and three missing, but I do not know that of the enemy. We paroled 700 of their wounded and left them at Winchester in their own hospitals, but I will not attempt any calculation of their loss from that data. The letter of a Northern correspondent at the time says: "Banks lost over two million dollars in property," and we know that Col. Connor, who was left by Jackson with one regiment at Front Royal, destroyed nearly $300,000 worth of property at that place when he was driven from there by McDowell in advance.

The Philistines had broken up the political Samson, but he "hadn't suffered defeat," so he told the secretary of war. I hope my readers will pardon my apparent exultation in passing over this part of the road, because I can't help being proud of the deeds my comrades did, and when I get to campaigning in memory's fields with "Stonewall the Great," my pulses quicken like a race-horse.

I don't mean any disrespect to anybody—but am a little like the old "grayback" who, after the surrender, went to the provost marshal, at Charlottesville, to be paroled. After taking all the oaths required of him, he asked the provost if he wasn't all right. "Yes," said the Captain, "you are." "Good a Union man as anybody, ain't I." "Yes," replied the Captain, "you are in the Union now as a loyal citizen, and can go ahead all right." "Well, then," said the old sinner, "didn't 'Stonewall' use to give us h—l in the Valley." You see he was one of "Stonewall's foot cavalry," and couldn't help being proud of it.

But I must return to the army of *generals* who were going to hold the Valley. We did hold it until the 30th of May, down at the bottom end of it—Charleston, Bunker Hill and vicinity—but a courier came to Gen. Jackson, and among other curious matters, related that Col. Connor's force at Front Royal had been captured by Gen. Shields, who was advancing by that route, that the "great pathfinder," Fremont, was moving from the west, both aiming to unite at Strasburg with a combined force of nearly forty thousand, which was interesting if true, and most of it proved true, for Jackson had only fifteen thousand effective men—all generals, however—and under the circumstances each general unanimously resolved to withdraw from the lower end of the Valley, if he could, and abandon for the present any further demonstrations on Harrisburg and Washington, thereby relieving those threatened points from the pressure which we had nearly resolved to bring upon them. In fact, the pressure appeared to have been, for the moment, applied in a totally different, and, to us generals, a very unexpected locality, for we had not had time in those four days' stay to familiarize ourselves with the capacity and resources of that part of the country. We managed to "hit the road" brisk enough to become familiar with *that* though, so much so that the last of us made fifty miles, walked too, from late in the afternoon of the 30th to the night of the 31st, which put us at Strasburg.

CHAPTER V.

On Sunday morning, June 1st, 1862, we walked out on the Wardonsville road and held service with Gen. Fremont's advance, which we checked, and finally drove his people back so far as to give us wagon room and let all our trains get safely past this dangerous point.

We fully expected Gen. Shields to take part in the exercises, which would have rendered them much more interesting to us, and knowing him to have been at Front Royal we knew it would be comparatively easy for him to do, but his failure to appear satisfied us that he had taken the Page Valley route, and now we were in for a race to New Market Gap. It is related, on good authority, that "once upon a time" a traveller found a boy, with hoe and crowbar, hard at work digging under a big rock, and inquired what he was after. "Ground-hog under here," was the sententious reply. "Do you expect to get him out?" asked the traveller. "*Expect to get him!*" said the boy—"*got* to get him; preacher be at our house to-day, and we're out of meat."

It was a "ground-hog case" now with "Stonewall," for this fourteen-mile wagon train carried the *visible* fruits of our victory over Banks, and we "*got* to get" to New Market Gap ahead of Shields or he'd cut our train off. We did get there, but it was a busy job, especially for Ashby and the rear guard, and the light batteries and sharpshooters kept up one continual roar all the way—day and night—as they contested, mile by mile, the advance of Fremont's column, which had taken the road in our rear when we left Strasburg. I don't believe he could have saved his train from us, if the conditions had been reversed, and Fremont had been conducting the retreat, with Jackson leading the advance, which brings up another pretty good war anecdote; whether true or not, makes no difference so far as the illustration is concerned:

During the long and bloody battle of Cold Harbour, between Grant and Lee, in '64, a Yankee soldier went to his Captain for a pass to army headquarters, saying he had a plan for ending the war, which he knew would work if he could get the authorities to adopt it, but he positively refused to communicate it to any but the commanding general. The Captain gave him the pass, and after considerable difficulty in keeping his secret, passed regimental, brigade, division and corps commanders, the soldier reached Grant's headquarters—and returned. His Captain observed that he seemed very much depressed in spirit, and promptly interviewed him as to the result of his mission, and by coaxing got a report. He said the General was absent when he reached headquarters, but the staff was so urgent, and made him believe that it was his duty to *immediately* give such important information to the chief that he did so. Here he stopped, but the Captain insisted upon knowing what occurred, and finally the man said: "Well, Captain, they don't want the war to stop nohow, for as soon as I told them my plan they kicked me out of the tent and kept it up for fifty yards, clear down to the woods; *and I came away.*"

"Now, then," said the Captain, "What was the plan you proposed?"

"Well, Sir," replied the soldier, "I told them to let Grant and Lee swap armies and the war would end in three weeks."

When we got to Woodstock we had to stop and give Fremont a lesson, but after passing Mt. Jackson and destroying the bridge over the Shenandoah, we knew we were clear—for the fluttering signals on the Massanutton told us that our cavalry had destroyed the White House bridge on the Luray road, and stopped Shields; so now "Stonewall" "like a wary lion," as Cooke puts it, slowly dragged his spoils to his lair, and although the enemy was up with us again we knew our trains were safe. At New Market we got the news of the battle at Seven Pines; the wounding of Gen. Johnson, and the assignment of Gen. R. E. Lee to the command of the Army of Northern Virginia. *The war had begun!*

We had another brush with Fremont, near Harrisonburg, on the 5th June, in which General Ashby was killed, which cast a gloom over the whole army, and was felt to be an irreparable calamity by every man in it. Our division, under Gen. Ewell, halted at Cross Keys, on the 7th, and made arrangements for battle. In the old times there had stood, at the intersection of several roads, an old-fashioned tavern, upon the swinging sign of which was painted two keys crossed, from which the name was derived; and now it was to be made famous by Ewell's fighting division, and given an enduring name on the page of history.

On Sunday, June 8th, 1862, we were ready again for our usual Sabbath exercises, and Fremont was on hand with his congregation. The 52d regiment got a fair share of business in this engagement, and lost a good many men. Major Ross was among the wounded, so was Lieut. Samuel Paul, of Company D, whose leg was shivered by a shell, within five steps of me, which caused amputation. He has since been treasurer of Augusta county, and I have often thought I would like to be treasurer of something myself—but all the one-legged Rebels can't get their living the same way, and Lieut. Paul—gallant soldier and good officer as he was—was equally as good a citizen, and deserves all the success he achieved. Lieut. King, of Company B, was killed here, and we were quite willing for Fremont's men to retire when they had got as much they wanted.

Our brigade was commanded in this battle by Gen. George H. Stuart, and was posted on the left centre of Ewell's line, sustaining and repulsing four distinct charges, each made by fresh troops; but they were mostly Dutch, and we fought them to the best advantage, behind trees, which Gen. Ewell's judicious selection of the ground gave us.

Fremont's Dutchmen were no match for the "foot-cavalry," and although Gen. Ewell himself says he had less than five thousand muskets, and Fremont's order of march, which was taken from an aid of Gen. Blenker killed by one of Trimble's men, showed six brigades, commanded by Blenker, Milroy, Stahel Steinwerh, and one other, of infantry, with one brigade of cavalry, numbering in all about twenty thousand, yet their dread of Jackson caused them to give way under slight pressure, especially when Gen. Trimble struck them in flank.

General Forrest, the famous cavalry commander of Tennessee, was once asked a question as to the cause of his almost constant success in his cavalry operations, when other commanders so frequently failed, and his answer was: "Well, I got thar first, with the most men;" and that in a sentence, gives the key to Jackson's generalship, if you add to it the Cromwellian motto, "Trust in the Lord, and keep your powder dry." We left the battle-ground of Cross Keys at midnight, and took the road to Port Republic, where Jackson, with his division, had been holding Shields in check; but the gallant Irishman was now coming on again in such force as to make a concentration of our forces necessary. Gen. Fremont reported his total loss at Cross Keys fight as two thousand, while Gen. Ewell's official report of our loss was three hundred killed, wounded, and missing; a very encouraging affair to Ewell's boys, who held the battle-ground, and equally discouraging to Fremont's who were forced to retreat.

The village of Port Republic lies in the angle made by the junction of the North and South rivers, which here form the south fork of the Shenandoah, along the east side of which Gen. Shields was moving. The Cross Keys road crosses the North river by a good bridge, into the town, and another road runs northeast from the town, by a ford in the South river, and down the south fork, by Conrad's store, to Luray. A third crosses at the same ford and running southeast, through Brown's Gap, in the Blue Ridge, leads to Charlottesville. I don't think it any harm to give this much geography, even if all my readers should also be posted in the big histories, but I am satisfied that many will read this who never saw any of the aforesaid big histories; and they will thus be better able to comprehend the successful performance of all the points of Jackson's magnificient strategy.

The position then was, Fremont at Harrisonburg, Shields at Conrad's Store — between which all the bridges were destroyed — and Jackson at Port Republic, forming a triangle, with sides fifteen miles long. Behind Jackson was the road through Brown's Gap, clear and open, so that he could fight them separately or fall back to Charlottesville and Richmond, and his operations up to this time had caused the troops of McDowell, Fremont and Shields to be withheld from McCellan, and at the same time put his own army within easy reach of Richmond should Gen. Lee desire his assistance.

Fremont with his 18,000, and Shields with his 15,000, would have been too much odds for Jackson's 12,000, to which he had been reduced since leaving Winchester; and he had no idea of permitting them to double on him, but he had got Fremont whipped by Ewell so easily, at Cross Keys, that he determined to double his own team and give Shields a trial. "Stonewall" was a thorough and consistent Christian, so far as I know, and was reported to do a great deal of praying, but he certainly did practice a great deal of deception on these two estimable gentlemen right here. We crossed the bridge over the North river early in the morning of June 9th, '62, and set it on fire as soon as everything was over—thus preventing Gen. Fremont from coming to Shields' assistance—but the ford of South river, owing to recent rains, was too deep for us, and we made a bridge of wagons and planks to get over on. Jackson's men were already engaged with the enemy and needed Ewell's assistance right away, and here was illustrated the influence of trifles on important events.

We could see the "Stonewall brigade" and Colonel Harry Hays' gallant 7th Louisiana, with the splendid batteries of Poague and Carpenter hotly fighting, but heavily overmatched, and we were hurrying as fast as we could to their assistance when a plank in our wagon-bridge slipped out, almost breaking up our means of crossing, and did delay us considerably, so much so that by the time we got over, formed our line and commenced our advance upon the enemy, we met Gen. Winder's troops retiring in confusion.

The 44th and 58th Va., by Gen. Ewell's directions, made a hot attack on the enemy's flank, but could not hold him long, and the whole line fell back to a piece of woods, losing one of Poague's 6-pounders and a good many men. Gen. Shields put a splendid 6-gun battery in a magnificient position to sweep the field, and I don't think he had an imported Dutchman in his army. They were all Western fellows, and stuck to their ground as if they belonged there, and it is my candid opinion that they were descendants of folks who had, years before, emigrated to the great West, from the Shenandoah Valley. Our advance, under Gen. Elzy, was through a fine field of wheat bordering on the river bottom, chin high, and their minnie balls clipped the grain worse than reapers. It was a very bad job of harvesting, the boys said—a harvest of death it proved—and much as we tried to make it short, the time dragged slowly enough, until it did seem that Shields was fully a match for "Stonewall" Jackson.

The two commanders manœuvered their men under fire, just as the old-time warriors used to do before long range weapons came into use, but still that terrible 6-gun battery held the key of the battle, and when Gen. Taylor rode up, Jackson turned to him and said: "Can you take that battery?—it must be taken!"

Taylor's answer was to gallop back to his brigade, and pointing with his sword to the enemy's guns, called out, in a voice like a bugle-blast, for thrilling wildness, "Louisianians, can you take that battery?" They answered, with a yet wilder thrill, "We're the boys can do that, General. You can bet on your boys!" and the gallant son of "Old Rough and Ready" led them forward.

Three times the Louisiana brigade drove the enemy back and captured the guns, but were as often repulsed, in turn, by the splendid soldiers of Shields. Taylor turned savagely for another trial, and Jackson seeing that Shields was heavily reënforcing his left to protect the battery, brought all he could to his own left, and as the Louisiana boys made thir last assault on the guns, threw all he had on Shields' right, breaking it all up, and at the same time Taylor took those dreadful guns, again turned them on the enemy, and the victory was won; but, as Cowan said to the devil—"'twas claw for claw," and we had fought as fine a body of troops as there was on the Continent, fully justifying the assurances of the 6th Louisiana— an Irish regiment—who said, when Fremont was beaten the day before, "This isn't much, but look out for tomorrow, for Shields' boys will be after fighting." The battle of Port Republic was one of the most sanguinary of the war, and we lost nearly a thousand men killed and wounded. I do not know the loss of the enemy in killed and wounded, but we captured 7 pieces of artillery with limbers and caissons, 975 prisoners, and more than 1000 small arms. One of the prisoners said to us—"You fired over our heads at Winchester, but you fired under them here."

Gen. Shields retired to Conrad's Store, but he was never routed, and stopped when Jackson did. He was badly crippled though, and Kernstown was atoned for, and the "Great Pathfinder," Fremont, was no longer able to act offensively in the Valley—except towards the citizens—but in this he was far superior in magnanimity to Milroy and others. General Shields was a favorite with the people among whom he operated, and treated them with consideration and kindness, but he was a terror when it came to fighting.

And now was accomplished the full purpose of "Stonewall's" strategy, for it was fully guaranteed that not another soldier could be spared from the defences of Washington to assist McClellan in the Chickahominy, because of the unknown motions of the man who could disappear and reappear so suddenly and unexpectedly, and while making such audacious marches right into the jaws of his powerful enemies, deliver such fearful blows and get out whole.

The very uncertainty and mystery which hung around him was worth an army, for it kept an army of the enemy unemployed while waiting for Jackson to develop his plan.

CHAPTER VI.

After Port Republic we enjoyed ourselves in our pleasant June camps about Mount Meridian, and began our planning and generalship again. There hadn't been quite so much of that among us since we left Strasburg, for the situation appeared to be mixed to such an extent that for some time each individual general had nearly decided that it would be as much as the bargain to get his own individual baggage out safe, but now we had shaken off the dogs of war which had howled at our heels and gnashed at our flanks like blood-hounds hunting the lion, and being free again were ready for a new campaign.

I think it best, from this time forward, to deal less in general history, if I can, so long as the war lasts, nd give my readers more of the incidents that clustered around the life of the soldier—but I couldn't help talking as I did about the Valley campaign; and how "Stonewall" was our hero and idol. His old, ambling sorrel, was, in our eyes, a war charger worthy of a Cœur de Lion; and his dingy coat and mangy cap were glorified. We didn't make game of him any more, but one irreverent fellow started, as a conundrum, "Why is Gen. Jackson a better leader than Moses was?" answering—"Because it took Moses forty years to march the children of Israel through the Wilderness, and Jackson would have double-quicked them through in three days." The army had suffered all the usual trials of military life—and death too—in time of war, and the men had been hurried by day and night; in storm and sunshine; in hunger and cold; on picket and camp guard; in the whistling tempest of lead, and the howling, demon shriek of shell; in the mangling of comrades, and the hasty burial of our dead on the field where they fell—and yet so wonderfully recuperative is the mind of man, that as soon as the pressure of adverse circumstances is removed, he lights his candle at the burning torch of hope and leaves the past all behind him. Just so did we, the men and boys, who had followed "Stonewall" through this trying campaign, come out bright and fresh, ready to follow again wherever the star of his destiny might lead—for we wanted to follow that destiny wherever it might be.

The brigade to which my regiment was attached was composed of the 13th Virginia regiment, made up of companies from the counties of Culpeper, Louisa, Orange, Frederick and Hampshire, and was commanded, during the war, by Colonels A. P. Hill, J. A. Walker and Terrell. The 31st Virginia, from Upshur, Randolph, Gilmer, Barbour and Highland, under Col. Hoffman. The 49th Virginia, from Rappahannock, Prince William, Fauquier, Nelson and Amherst, under Colonels Smith, (extra) and Gibson. And the 52nd Virginia—my own old "daisy" regiment—was from Augusta, Rockbridge and Bath, and had for Colonels, during the war, Baldwin, Harman, Watkins and Lilley. Our brigadiers were Edward Johnson, Elzey, Early, Pegram and Hoffman.

These were all gallant soldiers and good officers, whose names have gone into history gloriously, but "us boys" made the wreaths of fame that bound their brows, and we are proud that they wore them worthily.

A. P. Hill reached the rank of Lieut.-General, and was killed near Petersburg, by a straggler, just as the star of peace was breaking through the clouds; Terrell and Watkins were both killed, so was Board and Hoffman, now a judge in West Virginia, lost foot; but the old hero, Lieut.-General J. A. Early, more thoroughly lied on than any, and with more ability than all his traducers combined, is still among us; while Gibson, of Culpeper, is one of the most prominent lawyers of Middle Virginia, and may yet be Governor, carries on his person the scars of ten wounds received in battle. It used to appear very much as if fate, and not accident, had control of the bullets in battle, for some men went bravely through battle after battle with never a scratch to show for it, and were finally killed in some insignificant little skirmish, where not a dozen shots were fired; and then again there were men who would be wounded in very battle if they came in cannon shot of the field. I know one instance where as good a soldier as fought in the Southern army got hit with a ball every time he went into a fight, but not one serious wound among them, and his brother, in the same company, equally as good a soldier, who never missed a battle, went safely through the war with only one wound.

Some soldiers seemed to move in a charmed circle of safety, while others appeared to be bright particular objects of special favoritism when wounds were to be distributed, and in the latter part of the war the soldier was thought by his comrades to be especially lucky when he got a *furlough* wound—one that didn't quite kill, but allowed him to stay at home while it was healing.

We remained in the Valley long enough to get rested up good, and then moved through Brown's Gap, and "on to Richmond," for the new general of the army there was tired of McClellan's parallels, redoubts, salients and other engineering schemes on the Chickahominy, and desired to put a "Stonewall" across the road.

I remember picking up a Richmond paper about this time which contained a letter from a young lady in the country to her friend in the city, inviting her to pay a visit, and the ingenious working in of the names of our Generals interested me so much that I retained it in memory. The letter ran thus—

> "Come, leave the noisy *longstreet*,
> And come to the *fields* with me,
> Trip o'er the *heath* with flying feet,
> And skip along the *lea*.
> There *ewell* find the flowers that be
> Along the *stonewall* still.

    And pluck the buds of flowering pea
      That bloom on '*appy hill.*
    Across our *rodes* the *forrest* boughs
      A stately *arch*way form,
    Where sadly pipes the *early* bird
      Which failed to catch the worm."

Do for a school-girl pretty well I thought.

Coming out of the mountain pass we entered Albemarle county just when the cherries were ripe, and there were oceans of them, too. We got all we could of them, but time was too precious to waste in gathering cherries, for this march was to be made without the knowledge of the enemy, and in order to do this the soldiers were forbidden to tell the citizens what commands they belonged to, and were instructed to answer all questions in regard to the army with—"don't know."

The people all kept open house in Albemarle, and the "foot cavalry" enjoyed many a good, square meal among them. We sang the song of "Old Virginny Never Tire," and were very proud of our old State when the Alabama and Mississippi boys praised our people for their kindness and hospitality.

Gen. "Dick" Taylor tells of a breakfast he had with some old friends and relatives of his father in Orange county, on this march, which I think of sufficient interest to repeat in his own language:

"* * * That night we camped between Charlottesville and Gordonsville, in Orange county, the birth place of my father. A distant kinsman, whom I had never met, came to invite me to his house in the neighborhood. Learning that I always slept in camp, he seemed so much distressed as to get my consent to breakfast with him if he would engage to have breakfast at the barbarous hour of sunrise. His home was a little distant from the road, so the following morning he sent a mounted groom to show the way. My aide, young Hamilton, accompanied me, and Tom followed, of course. It was a fine old mansion, surrounded by well-kept grounds. This immediate region had not yet been touched by war. Flowering plants and rose trees, in full bloom, attested the glorious wealth of June. On the broad portico, to welcome us, stood the host with his fresh, charming wife, and, a little retired, a white-headed butler. Greetings over with host and lady, this delightful creature, with ebon face beaming hospitality, advanced holding a salver on which rested a huge silver goblet filled with Virginia's nectar, mint julep. Quantities of cracked ice rattled refreshingly in the goblet, sprigs of fragrant mint peered above its broad rim, a mass of white sugar too sweetly indolent to melt rested on the mint, and, like rosebuds on a snowbank, luscious strawberries crowned the sugar. Ah! that julep! Mars ne'er received such tipple from the hands of Ganymede! Breakfast was announced, and what a breakfast! A beautiful service, snowy tablecloth, damask napkins—long unknown; above all, a lovely woman in crisp gown, with more and handsomer roses on her cheek than in her garden. 'Twas an idyl in the midst of the stern realities of war! The table groaned beneath its viands. Sable servitors brought in, hot from the kitchen, cakes of wondrous forms, inventions of the tropical imaginations of Africa inflamed by Virginian hospitality. I was rather a moderate trencherman, but the performance of Hamilton was Gargantuan, alarming. Duty dragged us from this Eden; yet in the hurried adieus I did not forget to claim of the fair hortess the privilege of a cousin, I watched Hamilton narrowly for a time. The youth wore a sodden, apoplectic look, quite out of his usual brisk form. A gallop of some miles put him right, but for days he dilated on the breakfast with the gusto of one of Hannibal's veterans on the delights of Capua."

In order to the better understanding of the allusions to Hamilton and Tom, I will give the information that Lieut. Hamilton was a grandson of General Hamilton, of South Carolina, and was a cadet, in his second year, at West Point when the war commenced. Tom was the General's servant, three years his senior, and was his foster brother and early playmate. Tom's uncle, Charles Porter Strother, had been body servant to Gen. Zachary Taylor, following him in his Indian and Mexican campaigns, and Tom had served as aide to his uncle in Florida and Mexico. The General says Tom could light a fire in a minute, make the best coffee, and was superb at all manner of camp stews and roasts. He was an excellent horse groom as well as an expert at washing and ironing. He was always cheerful, but never laughed, and never spoke unless spoken to. Gen. Taylor thinks there was a mute sympathy between Gen. Jackson and Tom, and gives the following story in evidence of it:

He says he has often noticed them as they sat, silent by his camp fire, Jackson gazing abstractedly into the fire and Tom, respectfully withdrawn, gazing at Jackson. When Gen. Taylor's brigade went into action at Strasburg, he left Tom on a hill where all was quiet. After awhile, from some change in the enemy's dispositions, the place became rather hot, and Jackson, passing by, advised Tom to move; but he replied, if the General pleased, his master told him to stay there, and he would know where to find him, and he did not believe the shells would bother him. Two or three nights later, Gen. Jackson was at Taylor's camp fire, and Tom came up to bring them some coffee, whereupon Jackson rose and gravely shook him by the hand, and then told Gen. Taylor how Tom had held his position on the hill.

This little "side issue" to my story may not interest my readers, but it did me, very much, and I give it at a venture, and will now resume the march. Our objective point was Ashland, R. F. & P. R. R., and our route led us between the army of McDowell and the right wing of McClellan. As before stated, our Generals did not allow us to know anything at all, and so all us private generals gave the thing up and went ahead blindfold, with no guide but our unswerving faith in Gen. Jackson.

Some of the fellows had got on very familiar terms with him, indeed, so much so that they addressed him in common conversation as "Old Jack!" that is when he was not exactly present. When he *was* present it was our custom to throw up our hats and give him a rolling, rousing cheer, which usually had the effect to hurry him along, and I doubt very much if he liked it, for although he always took off his cap when passing this ordeal of homage, I noticed he got out of reach of it as fast as the "old sorrel" would take him.

But our pride in our general was still more increased when our sweeping fight, beginning at Mcchanicsville, brought the great, high generals of Lee's army over to our side of the Chickahominy to report to "Stonewall," and we saw Longstreet, A. P. and D. H. Hill, Hood, Branch, Stuart, Whiting and others, taking their orders gracefully from our great Valley chieftain; and we noticed the difference in their clothes, too, and notwithstanding they were better dressed, we could see a still brighter glow of glory over the damaged "duds" of *our* Jackson. We were proud of glorious "Old Dick" Ewell too, who took everything so calmly, *except when he was excited*, and was always ready just as he was in 1847 he led that squadron of Kearney's dragoons in their wild, dashing charge right up to the gates of the City of Mexico; but I want my reader not to forget that *our* "Stonewall" is the prince and hero of this little story as far as it has been spun yet, and I want them further to understand that the statements are historically accurate and correct to the best of my knowledge and belief. I don't think there can be any excuse for "knowingly or willingly" incorporating falsehohd in this little retrospective view, and if I do record anything not true, I do it unintentionally. There was but *one* Jackson.

This Chickahominy country is not much like the royal Valley of Virginia, and we always felt lost in it. No glimpse of the Blue Ridge charmed our eyes, nothing but flat, sedgy fields, piney woods with cypress trimmings, and scrubby, tangled mazes of wilderness, and swamps with stagnant, currentless streams of coffee-colored water. The air was not bracing and invigorating like our own grand, mountain country, but came lazily creeping through the woods and sedges in a languid, half-and-half style, and the whole thing bore on our spirits with a depressing influence. We missed the splendid, gushing springs of pure water we had always had at home, but never appreciated until now, and it gave us infinite trouble to rid ourselves of the ticks and chiggers that camped on us and entrenched themselves in our flesh. We knew that our depression was caused by the general sleepiness of this dreary, dismal country, which we had never seen before, for it resembles the whole Southern lowland country from which came those gallant regiments of North Carolina, Georgia, Mississippi, Alabama and Louisiana, that had helped us redeem the Valley, and the effect of our mountain air and water, with the magnificent views of our rolling Valley, and its clear, bright, rushing rivers upon those whole-souled Southern men was the very reverse of what this country had upon us, but our boys said it was all right for a battle-ground because it was impossible to spoil it, and it seemed fit for nothing else.

No Virginian of the Valley ever ought to make a home beyond the view of the mountains, for he will not be content, and will always feel an aching, longing to lay eyes on their billowy blue, no matter how long he may stay away from them. "Absence cannot conquer love."

"Bury me in the Valley of Virginia!" said "Stonewall" Jackson, on his deathbed; and not one of our boys but felt in their hearts the same desire, should the fate of war require the sacrifice of his life, but we didn't think as much of dying as the circumstances surrounding us justified; nor did the soldiers realize the nearness of death, when they were campaigning more than people do who plod along through their daily duty in the piping times of peace. As it had been in our Alleghany mountain campaign, in '61 with the names of mountains, streams and bridges, so now we learned new ones to us, and soon our tongue glibly rounded off, in conversation, a long string of local names, such as "Grapevine Bridge," "Bottom Bridge," "Long Bridge," "York River Railroad," "White House," "Pamunkey," "Williamsburg Road," "Charles City," "Nine Mile Road," "New Kent," "Hanover," &c. But there was *one* road, much mentioned too, which made an impression on the mind of the school-boy, and it was known all about as the "Darbytown Road," but spelled *Enroughty* road. Some of Fremont's Dutchmen might have managed to make " Darby" out of that conglomeration of letters, but " us boys " wasn't generals enough for that yet ; in point of fact we fell into line at once, as *full privates*, when we struck the " Enroughty-Darbytown Road," and obeyed orders just the same as if we had never held birthrights to generals' commissions.

Pawhick Creek was also a very interesting position to us, about the 27th June, for behind it, beyond the New Bridge road, we found the skilfully constructed fortifications which, with their massive banks of earth protected McClellan's men at the now doubly famous Cold Harbour.

In moving down from Mechanicsville to the York River R. R. we came to another of those sluggard streams, known as Tottapotamoi Creek, the bridge over which was burning, and we heard the enemy's axes chopping rapidly in the woods beyond, felling rces to obstruct our march, and making an almost solid barricade, but Gen. Hood put Riley's battery in position, and a few shells broke up the chopping so quick that when we again moved forward we found the axes sticking in the trees, but the choppers had disappeared. That day was as near perfect as it could be; air balmy, sky bright and cloudless, and nature doing her full share to make the "Old Virginia lowlands low," look decent, but we had not come down here to enjoy the scenery of nature, nor gather the delicious blackberries that lined the swamps and fields.

Just here I will introduce another extract from Gen. "Dick" Taylor, most astonishing I admit; and yet, from the high character of the evidence, not to be set aside without thought, but I must say that I have never, in all my reading of the history of the war, met anything like it:

"At the beginning of operations in the Richmond campaign Lee had seventy-five thousand and McClellan one hundred thousand, in round numbers—these figures taken from official sources. A high opinion has been expressed of the strategy of Lee, by which Jackson's forces were suddenly thrust between McDowell and McClellan's right, and it deserves all praise; but the tactics on the field were vastly inferior in the strategy. Indeed, it may be confidently asserted that from Cold Harbour to Malvern Hill, inclusive, there was nothing but a series of blunders, one after another, and all huge. The Confederate commanders knew no more about the topography of the country than they did about Central Africa. Here was a limited district, the whole of it within a day's march of Richmond, the Capital of Virginia and the

Confederacy, almost the first spot on the continent occupied by the English people * * * and yet we were profoundly ignorant of the country, were without maps or guides, and nearly as helpless as if we had been suddenly transferred to the banks of the Lualaba. The day before the battle of Malvern Hill President Davis could not find a guide with sufficient intelligence to conduct him from one of our columns to another. * * * For two days we lost McClellan's great army in a few miles of woodland, and never had any definite knowledge of its movements. * * * When it is remembered that Gen. McClellan's first operations in the Peninsula indicated the line of the Chickahominy as the most probable, for the defence of Richmond, the Confederate commander up to the battle of Seven Pines, Gen. Johnston, had been a topographical engineer in the U. S. army, while his successor, Gen. Lee, also an engineer, had been on duty at the War Office in Richmond, and in constant intercourse with President Davis, who was educated at West Point and served seven years * * * everyone must agree that our ignorance, in a military sense, of the battle-ground was simply amazing. * * * Gen McClellan was as superior to us in knowledge of our own land as were the Germans to the French in their war of 1870. * * * And so we blundered on like people trying to read without knowledge of their letters."

 I am not conceited enough to give any opinion of my own upon this subject even if I had one, but reading what Gen. Taylor has written, and reflecting upon it, calls to mind much that was nearly forgotten my revived memory can only account for many things that I saw in the military operations of the "Seven Days" by taking what he says as true. I now we had no pillar of cloud by day or of fire by night to lead us, but we also know that Gen. McClellan moved his army and trains by one single road after he commenced his retreat to the James, and only through ignorance somewhere on our part could he have accomplished it as successfully as he did. That Gen. Lee had beat him in strategy, and "wore out" his grand army with three men to his four is true, and that McClellan had previously determined, after Jackson's Valley campaign had locked up all his hoped for reenforcements, to change his base to the James River is also true, but that he was forced by inexorable fate, in the person of Lee, to make that change under pressure and before he was ready is as true as as any of it. And he was compelled to face his fate as best he could, but in doing it his army was ruined and the star of the "Young Napoleon" went down in blood among the Chickahominy swamps as the "Great" Napoleon's had done fifty years before amid the snows of Russia and the flames of Moscow.

The result had proved General Lee to be one of the greatest soldiers of history, and his throne in the hearts of his soldiers was thenceforward secure, but we do not want to lose sight of his admirable Lieutenants:—Longstreet, the "War Horse," as Gen. Lee called him, could always be relied on to hold the centre, where the hardest blows were given; and A. P. Hill, the dashing, chivalric, headlong commander of the "Light Division," who, always in feeble health, was never sick on battle days; Ewell, the blunt and fierce bulldog soldier, confided in by Jackson; Magruder, the boiling, tempestuous, enterprising leader Hood, the giant Texan, daring and indomitable "bravest of the brave;" Stuart, the prince of cavalrymen, chivalrous as a knight of the Round Table and all the way down the line, generals of divisions and brigades, colonels of regiments, commanders of squadrons and battalions, captains of companies, all coöperated with the troops; and the private soldier "the true hero of the war," without the incentive or motive which controls the officer, who hopes to live in history; without hope of reward, actuated only by duty and patriotism, he claimed the cause as his own and went into the war to "conquer or die," to be free or not to be at all.

History will yet award the chief glory where it belongs—to the private soldier. All these joined and executed the plans of Gen. Lee, which resulted in throwing Gen. McClellan's magnificent army back from the gates of the Southern capital, to tremble and cower beneath the guns of their fleet at Harrison's Landing, and the long agony was over. But we had met soldiers who "fought like brave men, long and well," and their army was not routed, though defeated.

We had won many trophies from our foes; embracing fifty pieces of artillery, many thousands of small arms, millions of dollars worth of property, and thousands of prisoners; but the supreme result was the deliverance of the city of Richmond.

It had cost us a heavy price to do this, and Jackson's men had poured out precious blood in the lowlands, as they had other precious blood in the Valley and among the Alleghanies.

Many of our gallant comrades slept their last sleep beneath the slopes of Hanover, in the gloomy swamps of the Chickahominy, and under the sighing pines of New Kent and Charles City.

> "Lowly they lie, forms of spirits departed;
> Lie, where in battle they struggled and fell,
> Unknelt by their graves, by the 'reft, broken-hearted.
> No marble enduring their noble deeds tell."

CHAPTER VII.

I am no statesman, nor do I wish to be considered one, but I think I represent the rank and file of the Southern Army, and will try, roughly, to tell what the private soldiers thought about the war, after a year's experience. We had our own ideas as to what it was for, and I know that the maintenance, or perpetuation of African slavery had no part in the motives which impelled us to endure the privations of the camp, the march, and all the tribulations which a state of war brought to us, including the danger and death of the battlefield. We did not think of slavery at all in connection with the war. Many of us did not think there was sufficient reason for the war anyway, and, like our old commander, Gen. J. A. Early, opposed secession as much, and as far as we could, but we were citizens of Virginia; we, who could, had voted for delegates to the State Convention with an honest determination—as good citizens—to abide by the result of their action. We believed the Federal Government was a creature of the States, ordained for the general good of all, but we felt that we owed paramount allegiance to Old Virginia, and when our State Convention, honestly and fairly elected, decided to withdraw the State from the Union, and their action was endorsed by an overwhelming majority of our people, we would have held ourselves to be traitors, ungrateful dogs, and death-deserving rebels, if we had failed to enlist under her "Sic Semper Tyrannis" banner.

We couldn't fight the Union and the State both, nor could we sit still and allow the Federal Government to throttle, stifle and crush our proud old Commonwealth, for doing that which we believed she had a perfect right to do, viz., resume all the rights and powers which she had delegated to the Federal Government. There had been no coercion used to compel her to enter the Union which, through her distinguished sons, she had been one of the foremost to promote, nor did we believe that our old-time fathers had knowingly bound her to a hateful partnership with a section bent on her ruin, by a tie which she had no right or power to sever.

We belonged first of all to Virginia, the blood of whose sons had in times past been shed from Quebec to Boston, from Boston to Savannah, for the liberty we enjoyed, and now where she required our services we, as loyal children, dared to go. And I know that for the first two years of the war slavery and its abolition did not draw the young men of the West into the Northern army, for I talked with many of them whom the fortune of war had made our prisoners, and without exception they declared they were fighting for the Union and the old Constitution, not to free the negro, who, they said, ought not to be free mong white people. Nor do I believe that Abraham Lincoln went into the war to free the slaves, at least he *said* he did not, and I believe he was honest, and m satisfied that if the South had surrendered any time during the first or second year of the war slavery would not have been abolished. The restoration of the *old* Union, under the old Constitution, would have left slavery intact, and in order to accomplish its entire removal it was necessary to establish a *new* covenant and *new* laws, which was ultimately done, but for four years we were the true defenders of the principles of the Constitution as it was, and if the states of the South had been guided by the counsels of that noble old Virginian, Henry A. Wise, and instead of secession had held on to the old flag, the equal rights of all the States, in the territories and elsewhere, would have been maintained, and the other fellows who equipped and sent forth John Brown on his mission of destruction would have been the rebels in the "irrepressible conflict."

But the hand of the God of Israel was in it, and he led us by a way that we knew not, through the flood and the fire, to the positive and emphatic removal of the disturbing elements which did so torment and distract us, and made the American Union of today—what it never was and never could be under the original confederation—*a nation!*

And now I know you will say I am wandering from my story, but before I return to "Stonewall," I will tell you of the famous "Louisiana Tigers," whose gallant commander, Major Wheat, was killed on the 7th June in the hottest of the fight at Cold Harbour. Nearly every account of the war which I have read by Northern writers gives great prominence in every battle to the "Tigers," and I am of the opinion that every soldier in the Union army actually thought he fought the "Tigers." I cannot estimate the number they must originally have mustered, according to the amount of fighting they are represented by the boys in blue to have done, but there was certainly more than a million of them, or they wouldn't "go around." It is something like the Yankee boys at Gettysburg where every mother's son of them fought and slew the men of "Pickett's Division," and also a little like the "Gray Jackets" who are fond of detailing desperate combats with the "Pennsylvania Bucktails." Nearly every regiment in Lee's army has, on one or more occasions, "locked horns" with the "Bucktails." It is unquestionably a compliment to the "Tigers," to "Pickett's Division," and to the "Bucktails," to be selected as special antagonists by men who were hunting "foemen worthy of their steel," but it is a fact that "Pickett's Division" at Gettysburg did not number five thousand, and on the authority of General "Dick" Taylor, who was their brigade commander as long as they had an organization, will now tell who and what the "Tigers" were:

Before the first battle of Mañassas there were some three companies from Louisiana unattached to regiments that were thrown together as a battalion. The strongest of the three, and giving character to all, was called the "Tigers," and was recruited on the levees and in the alleys of New Orleans, and might have come out of "Alsatia," where they would have been most worthy subjects of "Duke Hildebrod." This company was raised and commanded by Wheat himself in the beinning, but on the formation of the battalion and his promotion to major it was under Capt. White, a man of many *aliases* and unsavory character, and so villainous was the reputation of this battalion that no brigadier desired the honor of commanding it, but by hard discipline and some executions by sentence by court-martial, Gen. "Dick" got them in some sort of subjection, but he says they always would plunder in spite of his orders, unless he was with them in person, at every battle. His account of them the 24th of May, '62, when with Jackson at Front Royal, reads like this:

"In the morning Jackson led the way; my brigade, a small body of cavalry, and a section of the Rockbridge battery formed the column. Major Wheat, with his battalion of "Tigers," was directed to keep close to the guns. Sturdy marchers, they trotted along with the cavalry and artillery at Jackson's heels, and after several hours were some distance in advance of the brigade, with which I remained. A volley in front stirred us up to a "double," and we speedily came upon a moving spectacle. Jackson had struck the Valley pike at Middletown, along which a large body of Federal cavalry, with many wagons, was hastening north. He had attacked at once with his handful of men, and overwhelming resistance, had captured prisoners and wagons. The gentle 'Tigers' were looting quite merrily, diving in and out of wagons with the activity of rabbits in a warren; but this occupation was abandoned on my approach, and in a moment they were in line, looking as solemn and virtuous as deacons at a funeral."

The redoubtable Major Bob. Wheat was always a

character in war, if there *was* any war anywhere. The son of an Episcopal clergyman, he ran off from school and followed Gen. Zachary Taylor through the battles of Palo Alto, Resaca de la Palma, and Monterey, until he was badly wounded. After the Mexican war he went with Lopez to Cuba, where he was wounded in a desperate fight with the Spanish troops and captured, but his guardian angel saved him, somehow, from the garrote, which crushed the necks of all his comrades in this reckless enterprise, and he escaped to follow Gen. Walker, the "gray-eyed man of destiny," in his fillibuster expedition to Nicaragua, where the incapacity of the South American patriots so disgusted him that he left them to their vacillations; and crossing the Atlantic, he joined Garibaldi, in Italy, in whose army of ragamuffins he did noble service in the cause of liberty; but his keen scent of war brought him home to America, early in '61, in time to catch a bullet at first Manassas. At Harrisonburg, Va., on the 5th June, '62, where Gen. Ashby was killed; and one of the last dashes he made, with his famous cavalry, was to capture Col. Sir Percy Wyndham, of Fremont's cavalry; Col. Wyndham was brought to the rear a prisoner. No one knew him, but the troops jeered at him, some, as the big "*Yankee* Colonel," and the Colonel, being an Englishman, hated the name of *Yankee* worse than anything else, which caused a fearful scowl to settle on his features. As soon as Wheat laid eyes on him, he sprang from his horse with a glad cry of, "Why Percy! old boy! where did you come from?" at the same time throwing his arms around the Colonel' neck; and Wyndham, with a responsive thrill, exlaimed, as he returned the embrace of his old-time mess-mate in the Garabaldi wars: "Why, Bob! God bless you; *is* this you?" Nobody applied the insulting epithet of *Yankee* to Col. Wyndham again, while Major Wheat was about.

The gallant Bob. Wheat met his death as before stated, in the battle of Cold Harbour, just at sunset, and the last words from his lips were, "boys, we've won the fight, bury me on the field!"

With Major Wheat gone no one could hold his men together, and the Louisiana Tigers, in *fact*, ceased to exist, but the Northern soldiers, in *fancy*, continued to fight the Tigers for two years more.

We will now return to "Stonewall" near Richmond, his army merged into the A. N. V., waiting for McClellan to get reënforcements and rest up his Army of the Potomace for another movement against our modern Rome, the seven-hilled city on the James.

About this time we began to tremble for our cause, in consequence of the fearful disasters about to be brought upon this devoted army of martyrs by the *Pope*. Not the gentle Roman pontiff, Pius IX, but a greater than all pontiffs combined, to-wit.: Major-General John Pope, U. S. A., commanding the "Army of Virginia." This most wonderful, all-conquering, and invincible commander, had come, as he informed us in general orders, from the West, where he had never seen any more of his enemies than their backs, and the common idea of his own folks was that the spirit of Julius Cæsar: *veni, vidi, vici,* and all, had been again incarcerated in John Pope, Major-General. It was, moreover, a matter of scientific knowledge to the most eminent astrologers, that the planets, Jupiter and Mars, were in conjunction at the precise moment of his birth. The regular astronomer of his native town had requested that he be christened "Jupiter Mars" Pope, which would have looked remarkably well at the foot of a general order issued from " H'd Q'rs in the the saddle," but his parents were afraid to risk it. Still, the more ordinary name of "John," with which he was invested, did not prevent his development into a mighty man for thunder. No question as to the location of his "headquarters" could ever arise, for he tells us himself that they are "in the saddle ;" an eminently proper location for the headquarters of a commanding general of the army, for the reason, that in the event of small parties of the enemy's cavalry demonstrating in the neighborhood, the headquarters can be moved with promptness and facility.

The portions of the general orders which caused us most concern were those bearing directly upon our own conduct, as Rebels, because he fulminated so fiercely against stray rebels committing "overt acts of war" upon any, or sundry sutler wagons, horses or what not ; and in case we should in anywise be thus guilty of depredations, in the limits of his department, no less than five Southern citizens were to be held accountable, in each instance in their persons goods, and chattels. He was *particularly* sever. upon the citizens in the matter of "overt acts of war committed by Rebel soldiers, and we grew very uneasy, lest Jackson, or Ewell, or somebody, migh lead us into some indiscretion which the "Major General commanding Army of Virginia," migh construe into an "overt act," &c. We had bee watching "Stonewall" pretty closely, and noticing that he did not read the papers of the day, we feared he might, through ignorance of the General's general order, do something which we should all regret, as being distasteful to Major-General Pope.

Another clause of "general orders" also gave us great uneasiness, and we were glad Jackson did *not* read the papers, when this came to our knowledge, but self-respect required, as we thought, some action in regard to it at our hands. The Major-General, in his clause, applied some very ugly names to us—in fact—he called us "disaster and shame," and we knew he had particular reference to Jackson's men, for his language was, that "disaster and shame," as aforesaid, "lurked in the rear;" and it was generally known that "Stonewall" was a bad man for lurking in the rear; but we had never had such epithets applied to us before, by any of the commanding generals, not even Banks. We consulted and took counsel together—we generals of the rank and file—but we couldn't exactly determine what to do about it; whether to write to Major-General Pope asking him to modify his severe language, or to disband and go to Texas, singly or in pairs, as would be most expedient. We remained in this state of doubt and uncertainty, not unmixed with dread until the 19th July, 1862, when "Stonewall" roused up, shook his mane, growled a little, and started towards Gordonsville. We did all we could to persuade him against "lurking," but we went along, for we couldn't think of permitting him to get out of our sight, for fear he might do some "overt act," and about this time we got some more news from Gen. Pope which rendered it doubly important for us to keep an eye pretty closely on Jackson. The "Major-General commanding," had been before the congressional committee on the conduct of the war, and had there declared that, "with such an army as McClellan had in March, '62, he would engage to sweep the country from Washington to New Orleans," and we estimated that if the U. S. Government should give him such a one we would hardly be safe in Texas.

When we reached Gordonsville it became necessary to learn positively the whereabouts of the "Army of Virginia," and it was not very long until we had it located. We found it particularly active in Madison and Orange counties, engaged in heavy forays on citizens and their property of every description; and when Major-Gen. Pope had swept the country to the Rapidan the most noticeable result of his victorious march was the complete stamping out, in the minds of the inhabitants of the conquered territory, of the heresy of secession. One of his staff officers reports stopping at a house in Culpeper where the family was just sitting down to dinner, and in fifteen minutes the soldiers had not only swallowed the dinner but had swept up and carried away everything portable or eatable, live-stock and all, indoors and out, and a little son of the proprietor said to this staff officer, "Pap says he wouldn't vote the secession ticket again if he had the chance," which, the officer said, was extremely gratifying to him.

The reconversion of the territory from treasonable proclivities to loyalty was, of course, equal in extent to the spread of the wings of his army—which was from the Blue Ridge to the junction of the rivers

Rapidan and Rappahannock, and it was only necessary to continue the movement to the Gulf of Mexico in order to completely restore the love of the Union in the hearts of all the people. A Northern correspondent who accompanied the army wrote: "The land was green when they came, but they left a desert behind them;" and Gen. Pope, to more fully establish loyalty in his department, issued what he called his expatiation order, which required that "all male citizens disloyal to the United States should be immediately arrested, the oath of allegiance proffered them, and if they took it *and furnished sufficient security for its observance*, they should be released. If they declined taking it they should be sent beyond the extreme Federal pickets, and found again within his lines should be treated as spies and shot." Another order had a very salutary effect on the home folks, which was, that "the prominent citizens of the district should be arrested and detained as hostages for the good behavior of the inhabitants, and made to suffer in their persons for the acts of partizans and bushwhackers." If any of the Federal troops were "bushwhacked," one of the hostages should suffer death.

All this and much more us generals had on our minds to distract us, and it made us still anxious to prevent Gen. Jackson from committing depredations in the army lines of Gen. Pope, so that we lost a good deal of sleep watching him. We kept all such information from him as much as possible, knowing, from the nature of the man, that if he should get full accounts of Pope's proceedings it would excite him, and perhaps cause him to commit some "overt act."

However, some indiscreet person gave him a newspaper one day, and then the " fat was in the fire," and we gave up the idea of being generals any more until *somebody* should get " wore out."

Jackson crossed the Rapidan at Barnett's ford on the 8th August, and marched us steadily forward towards Culpeper C. H., right into the jaws of destruction " us boys " thought. The next day we reached Cedar Run, eight miles from the C. H., and right here we came square up against the centre of Major-Gen. Pope's army. How I wish he had been named " Jupiter Mars " for plain " John " seems too plain and simple and naked to clothe the Julius Cæsar of North America. Anyhow, " Stonewall " drove his wedges right into the centre of the " Army of Virginia," which here consisted of 32,000 men, according to official reports of Major-Gen. J. Pope, but we soon learned from prisoners that Gen. Banks was in command here, and the horizon began to clear, for we knew if that was the case that we wouldn't go to Texas yet awhile. We didn't believe Gen. Banks could drive Jackson out of Culpeper if Pope would give him the job.

We got to business on the 9th, about the middle of the afternoon, and after considerable skirmishing and cannon-firing Gen. Early moved his brigade along the Culpeper road, drove the enemy's cavalry before him, and pushed his line to the crest of a hill but the Federal batteries opened such a furious cannonade upon the hill that he withdrew his troops below the crest and hurried up his own batteries to reply. A large body of cavalry appeared on our left flank, and we fixed ourselves to attend to them, but

Captains Brown and Dement opened on them with their batteries which settled that matter pretty soon. While all this was going on, Gen. Winder, with Jackson's old division, moved upon our left, and a column of Federals made a drive straight at our batteries, but Gen. Early put his whole line forward, and the battle was joined along our entire front, and raged furiously till night.

Jackson's army was composed of his own division, commanded by Winder; Ewell's division, and part of A. P. Hill's. Gen. Thomas' brigade, of Hill's, came to Gen. Early's support just when we needed help; and we succeeded in driving them to the woods, where they held on for awhile, but finally a general charge swept them through the woods and away towards the C. H. They made a last attempt to drive us back with cavalry, but Taliaferro and Branch ruined them, and their dashing charge ended in a rout, leaving Gen. Price, their commander, a prisoner. We had 223 killed and 1,060 wounded. I don't know the enemy's loss, but we got over 400 prisoners, 5,300 small arms, one Napoleon gun and caisson and the caissons of two other guns. We had given Major-Gen. J. Pope's army a trial and had come out "on top." Our infantry had beaten his fairly in the open field, giving them a choice of position, and our artillery had outshot his.

It is not hard for one who is engaged in a battle to comprehend a written description of it, but these descriptions are not often written by men who were actually engaged in the line of battle.

The soldier sees very little of the general engagement, and when he attempts to describe the field he does so on other people's information, not his own knowledge. A battlefield, where only five or ten thousand troops are engaged, is a much more extensive area than most people suppose, and when large bodies of soldiers—say fifty thousand on a side—are in it, a man on a good horse could hardly gallop from point to point, over the whole field, during the continuance of the battle. The field is large, but each soldier only knows what is being done in his own vicinity, generally, the space occupied by his own company, and sometimes not that much.

When we are preparing for the battle you will notice that the columns, which have been moving steadily forward all day halt, and seem to hesitate like a swarm of bees, whether to light or not ; whether to go forward or back. The men don't ask, "what's the matter," for they know, most of them, exactly what it is, and the old infantry soldier don't need anybody to tell him when he is on the edge of a battle They notice that the Colonels are talking with the Generals, and they see officers and couriers galloping some towards the front and others to the rear. The infantry open their columns, and the cavalry, with jingling spurs and clanking sabres, trot forward. The ammunition wagons roll heavily up, and the ambulances move along, the surgeons chatting cheerfully with each other, and the men are all jokey and chatty There is a good deal of handling of field glasses by the general officers, and the Colonels and Captains show a good deal of cool, calm anxiety to have their men well in hand. No hurrying or confusion about it, not so much as if they were going out on a review but it seem to do them good to see the boys cheerfu

art. After awhile somebody rides up
ɔking Colonel, on the gray horse, and
ds, and he turns around to the regi-
ort, prompt manner, and says quietly,
sharp: "Attention, 21st," or whatever
y be—"forward!" and away goes the
nt to the front. You can see them
 and strong in column, for a bit, and
 the Colonel say, "front into line,
on they go, up the hill to the fence,
jump over, and you hear the guns—
g! bang! the familiar "Rebel yell"
id the firing grows in volume—quick,
. You, perhaps, think this is a battle,
t would pass for one in Revolutionary
only skirmishers advancing now, and
 cheerfully, about ten or fifteen feet
d loading rapidly, calling funny re-
other, laughing, shouting and cheer-
cing. Some of them drop out of the
) the rear, some lay flat on the ground,
lly hurt to travel, but the line moves
same and the vacant places are filled
ving over to the right or left, and pre-
ch the timber, where every man posts
 a tree, stump, rock, anything that
and, in the most deliberate manner
ring, which now changes its rattling
ng like a roar, but it is not a battle
's have only driven the enemy's skir-
ɔn their line of battle, and developed
and now a battery gallops up and
ɔsition, unlimbers the heavy trails and

the Captain commands: "Commence firing." The artillerymen step in briskly and cheerfully, and load the pieces, then step aside; a blaze of fire flies from the muzzle of the first gun, in a puff of white smoke, and away goes a howling shell, over the heads of the skirmish line, to explode in the enemy's line, and you hear that yell again. Gun after gun blazes forth its shrieking shell with all the rapidity possible, sometimes so fast as to fire three rounds a minute from each gun, and all the while that skirmish line is "pop! pop! bang! banging away!" Now comes another movement, as the brigade forms up in line; a thousand, yes, two thousand ramrods rattle down into the barrels of as many muskets! then the long drawn command, "forward!" rings down the line, and the skirmishers are relieved, but not a minute too soon, for they have been compelled to lie down flat on the ground, with their heads against the trees in front, unable either to advance or retire without meeting certain death, but when their brigade line comes up, they yell with joy, pride, excitement, jump to their feet and charge right on with the "old brigade;" for they are proud of *their* "old brigade." It may be known along the line as "Early's or Taylor's, or Winder's, or maybe the 'Stonewall' brigade," but those men know it as "*our* brigade," and now you are safe in reporting that the battle has begun.

The sharply sparkling, rattling roar of the rifles of the skirmishers is swallowed up in the rolling, booming thunder of the musketry, which, in tone like a mighty, rushing wind, rises, swells, lulls, and roars again along the line, and now it is that the spectator, who is viewing his first battle, thinks, as the smoke-loud rolls up above the trees and he hears the horribly crashing volleys blending together, that no man can be left alive. It is a busy time, and the couriers, aides and staff officers gallop and dash from place to place on foaming steeds, bearing orders along the hotly-contested line. Brigades and divisions wheel into position and press forward, and blazing batteries crown every hill. The ammunition wagons get up, somehow, in reach of the troops, and the light riding, empty ambulances spin along, right up to the line of fighting, soon to return, solemnly moving to the rear with their ghastly loads of mangled soldiers, while the shells and bullets fly about in an indiscriminate, aimless sort of way, anywhere at all, and are liable to hit anybody at all. Now the enemy's batteries are in position and warmed to their work, and the "sulphurous canopy" darkens all the field and forest for miles, the musket-balls rap and whack on the guns and cannon wheels, while occasionally a caisson of artillery ammunition is blown up by an exploding shell, and the burned and mangled bodies of the men near it whirl up into the air. The battle is in full blast now, and the time has come to test the metal and discipline of the troops, but if "Stonewall" is on the field we will soon hear a roll of musketry or crashing battery roar away off on the flank or rear of the sturdy fighting blue line in our front, and soon we see their batteries limber up hastily and gallop back; for the guns must be saved, at all risk; then their infantry line slowly gives ground, and our cannoniers break out into a wild cheer, which is taken up by the infantry, and the shout of victory rings gloriously, up through the smoky pall, from the thousands of throats that we thought awhile ago were all stilled in death. And here comes the cavalry, in columns and squadrons, galloping after the retiring enemy, charging into their cavalry and light batteries, which are covering the retreat. This keeps up for long distances, generally, and we see the streams of wounded men, and parties of dejected looking prisoners coming back, with perhaps a captured cannon, and wagons now and then, for defeat and rout means irretrievable ruin to the army that suffers it, if our "Stonewall the great" commands the army that wins.

But this last part is about all the private soldier sees of a battle. However, after it is over, each man tells his neighbor what he saw, and by tomorrow each one of us imagines he saw the whole battle, for it is a rare school for the cultivation of imagination; and we tell the whole story—thus picked up and patched together—until *some* of *us*, after awhile, *swear* to being an eye-witness to every scene and movement of that battle; nor can you blame us, for it is not every one that can go through a four-year experience like that and be able to tell about it afterwards, and the stirring times of that war made a deep impression on our minds, but we old veterans are growing old, our ranks are thinned and thinning, and soon we'll cross over to camp with the majority. To this new man, who has just got a glimpse of his first battle, one of the strangest things is the cheerfulness of the soldiers under fire, and their general jollity amid the hailstorm of battle. He wonders how that artilleryman at Gettysburg, while doing his duty at his gun in the battery, could sing, as he did—

his comrade, near, respond—"Yes, and a gallant at that."

We have an anecdote, well vouched for, of a gallant sergeant, in a Union regiment, in one of the Wilderness battles. A rebel battery was spreading havoc over the field and the General ordered the Colonel to take it. The Colonel turned to his regiment and exclaimed, "Men, the General says he wants that battery. Can't we take it for him?" This sergeant stuttered, or stammered, some folks call it: said he, "S-s-say—Colonel—l-l-let's t-t-take up a c-c-collection and b-b-buy the b-bl-blamed thing. I'll th-throw in my sh-share," but we are told that the regiment did take the battery, and the sergeant did his duty no less manfully and bravely, for his joke.

CHAPTER VIII.

Now I must go back to my hero, "Stonewall the Great," for he is about to make another "lurking" expedition to the "rear" of Major-Gen. John Pope, inasmuch as Gen. Lee has moved the whole army up from Richmond and "us generals" have determined to do what we can for the "Army of Virginia" before the "Army of the Potomac" can reach it, for we don't care to yoke up to Gen. McClellan right away. He gave us all we wanted from him in that last interview at Malvern Hill, and we had much rather fight the great annihilator, Major-Gen. Pope, now that we have got his measure, than bother with "Little Mac." We had been loafing around in Orange county since Cedar Run until July 1st, when we moved up to Mt. Pisgah church. Gen. Jackson now had under his command—1st, Ewell's division, composed of the brigades of Lawton, Early, Trimble and Hays, with the batteries of Brown, Dement, Lattimer, Balthus and D'Aquin ; 2d, A. P. Hill's division, of the brigades of Branch, Gregg, Field, Pendar, Archer and Thomas, and the batteries of Braxton, Latham, Crenshaw, McIntosh, Davidson and Pegram; 3d, Jackson's old division, under Brig.-Gen. W. B. Taliaferro, with the brigades of Winder (Col. Baylor); Campbell (Maj. Seddon); Taliaferro (Col. A. G. Taliaferro); and Starke, with the batteries of Brockenborough, Wooding, Poague, Caskie, Carpenter and Raines. The cavalry of Gen. Stuart was everywhere, front, flank and rear, and were continually doing some "overt act of war" to the annoyance and displeasure of Major-Gen. Pope, and right in his department too, where he found himself utterly unable to control the operations of these rough-riders by arresting and holding citizens responsible for depredations by soldiers against his troops and trains.

Some Federal cavalry played a splendid joke on Stuart himself by surprising him at Vidiersville while he was at breakfast, and causing him to mount his horse in haste and gallop off bare-headed, while they retired in triumph, carrying off his hat, cloak and haversack. It was the first time Stuart was ever "caught napping," and "his wreath had lost a rose," but he made it bloom again a few days after by a gallant foray in Pope's rear at Catlett's Station, where he captured his headquarter wagons with the " great annihilator's " money-chest, dispatch book, and hat with its ostrich plume, and Stuart was himself again.

I wish I could drop the generalities of history and move along as I should with the "shameless" disaster hunting gray-jackets of "Stonewall," but I must keep up. We moved on 20th August from Mt. Pisgah, by way of Somerville ford, to Stevensburg, in Culpeper, and now we were almost in Major-Gen. Pope's trap, for he had said "publicly" that "he did not intend to take any step backward," and if he shouldn't, and Jackson kept on advancing, it was very clear that we would have to join Pope or break up before long. His columns were very numerous, and his batteries crowned every hill on the other side of the Rappahannock, but in spite of it all we moved up to Beverley's ford on the 21st, and all day long the booming cannon and bursting shells kept up the concert. On the 22d we moved up the river, over the Hazel to Freeman's ford, but this was strongly guarded too, so we went on to Warrenton Springs. Gen. Jackson had evidently been reading another newspaper, and it looked to us now as if he was bent on finding out if Pope had any rear.' Gen. Early crossed the river here with his brigade, and, by the way, it is a noticeable fact that both Lee and Jackson were prompt to select our brigadier, "Old Jubilee," as his men called him, for delicate and dangerous operations; but the rains descended and the floods came, and it looked mighty dark for Early, with only one brigade, in the midst of the whole army of the "Great Annihilator," and cut off from all help by the foaming, bankful Rappahannock, but he held out till Jackson got a bridge built, and came out of the lions' den, like Daniel of old, with never a scratch on him.

Gen. Lee, by aid of the papers and order-book of Pope, brought in by Stuart when he went after his hat, now planned a magnificent scheme for flanking towards the left and getting in the enemy's rear, and of course "Stonewall" must lead the movement, and away we went on Monday, 25th August, through Amissville, over the river at Hinson's ford, by Orleans, in Fauquier, to Salem, on the M. G. R. R.

I have before alluded to the reprehensible practice of deception by this "blue light" Presbyterian elder in his military operations, but on this occasion he out-did himself, and grossly deceived John Pope— Major-General, &c.—as to his real purpose. He gave out, incidentally, that he was moving to the Valley; and, to fix this impression in the mind of the great commander of the "Army of Virginia," who was "careless of lines of retreat," and who "took no step backwards," he sent out couriers with curiously written dispatches to the effect that his movement was a Valley one, and actually caused these couriers to take routes by which he knew *some* of them would be captured, and their papers fall into the hands of Gen. Pope, which actually occurred, and by such false pretenses relieved that great General's mind of any further trouble in regard to the Rebel column, which his signal posts reported to be moving towards the Blue Ridge. It was a *moving* column, truly, and taking "nigh cuts," across lots, we got to Salem at midnight, without a straggler, and still marching. On the 26th we walked through Thoroughfare Gap and "lurked," with "disaster and shame," right down on Manassas Junction, leaving Maj.-Gen. Pope still operating on the Rappahannock, under the deluded

ea that Jackson had run off to the Valley, and he
as about to dispose of what Rebels were left in his
ont, take Richmond, and sweep right on to New
rleans.

> "At midnight in his guarded tent,
> The Turk was dreaming of the hour," etc.

ut—

> "At midnight in the forest shades,
> Bozzaris ranged his Sulite band."

History repeats itself, and we have only to wait to
e that — "the thing which is, is that which hath
en, and there is no new thing under the sun."
We had marched fast and long, and had also *fasted*
ng, but when the vast magazines of supplies, cap-
red right between Pope and Washington City, were
ened to us, the boys hardly knew what to lay
nds on first in the way of eatables. No pen can
scribe the rollicking antics of Jackson's men, as
ey revelled among the good things spread in prodi-
l profusion around them—in army goods and sut-
r stores. It was more than funny to see the ragged,
ugh, dirty fellows, who had been half living on
asted corn and green apples, for days, now drinking
hine wine, eating lobster salad, potted tongue, cream
scuit, pound cake, canned fruits, and the like; and
ling pockets and haversacks with ground coffee,
oth-brushes, condensed milk and silk handkerchiefs.
he captures at Manassas are thus summed up, in
eneral Jackson's report: "Eight pieces artillery,
venty-two horses and equipments, three hundred
isoners, two hundred negroes, two hundred new
nts, one hundred and seventy-five extra horses, ten
comotives, two railroad trains loaded with stores

worth several millions of dollars, 50,000 lbs. bacon, 1,000 barrels of beef, 20,000 barrels pork, several thousand barrels of flour, and a very large quantity of sutler's stores." The folks at Washington made an effort to save it, by sending Gen. Taylor, with his brigade of New Jersey troops, by rail, to drive us away; but the "Old Blue Hen's Chickens" were not strong enough to whip the "Stonewall Gray Jackets" out of that place, for we got together, with our guns, killed the General and tore the brigade to atoms. Jackson always said his men would fight for something to eat.

This was the morning of the 27th., and we pretty soon learned that Gen. Pope had been notified that his army supplies, "in his rear," were in danger, for his whole army came trooping back in clouds, and we had to pack up and move out. So we filled up all we could carry of the good things and fired the balance. It was hard on us to see so much good eatables burned up, but it made a splendid blaze, and we knew Pope's army couldn't fight without rations. Of course all manner of rumors and reports were flying around among the soldiers, and we believed all we heard—a little—but most of them were spoken of "reports by *grapevine* telegraph," an expression denoting lack of faith in their reliability; and, speaking of the telegraph reminds me of the prompt action taken by a keen cavalryman of, I think, Col. Munford's regiments, at Manassas. He had never seen a telegraph instrument before, and came upon one here which was ticking away in fine business style, and, his excited imagination, it was some "infernal machine" arranged to explode the magazine or some

ing, and perhaps kill the whole army. Taking the
 atter and its consequence in at a glance, he gallantly
 solved to sacrifice himself to save his comrades,
 d springing upon it, with the suddenness of a tiger,
 kicked the mysterious ticker to atoms with his
 g boots, and rushing out of the office, exclaimed—
 Boys! they was a tryin' to blow us up, but I seen
 eir triggers a workin' and busted 'em."

About this time Pope began to use his "grapevine
 legraph" quite freely, and when Gen. Ewell used
 e 6th and 8th Louisiana regiment and the 60th
 eorgia, at close range, to hold the two leading
 igades of the Federal army in check, until the
 uff at Manassas was all destroyed—and held his
 ound so obstinately, by aid of the cavalry regi-
 ents of Colonels Munford and Rosser, (2nd and 5th
 irginia), that Pope got his army in line for a general
 igagement, when Ewell withdrew his little force,
 aving Gen. Early, with his brigade and the cavalry,
 protect his rear, and retired to Manassas; Gen. Pope
 imediately telegraphed to Washington that he "had
 uted and cut off Jackson and his whole force;"
 hich was fully believed all over the North, and not
 ng afterwards he telegraphed to Baltimore to "make
 om for Jackson and 16,000 prisoners," which he
 had bagged," as he called it.

The Federal army could not stand the destruction
 stores at Manassas, and when Fitz. Lee struck out
 r Fairfax C. H., with his cavalry, preventing supply
 ains coming from Washington, Pope was in a con-
 tion to be starved in the open field, something
 most unheard of in military history of superior
 mies, and his main apology—apart from the Fitz-

John Porter "scape-goat" business—for his defeat at Manassas was the want of rations for his men and forage for his horses.

It always seemed to the folks who were looking at the campaign the "invincible annihilator" of Lee's army was premature in "discarding lines of retreat and bases of supplies" so promptly in the beginning of his operations, because we all thought "Stonewall" was the man to attend to those little matters for him; and the shadow of Jackson did rest heavily on Pope's army when it entered Manassas on the 28th August.

At this time, while fighting and manœuvering to hold our own until Gen. Lee could get to us with the balance of the army, a shell was thrown into our ranks from the Warrenton Road, exploding in Company C, of the 52d Regiment, which killed and wounded eighteen men, seven of them being killed on the spot. Among the wounded by this fatal shell was Col. James H. Skinner, of Staunton, Va., commanding the regiment. Col. Skinner was afterwards wounded at Gettysburg by a shell which exploded on the ground in front of him, and blinded for several months by the dirt and gravel thrown into his eyes. In the battle of Spottsylvania C. H., Col. Skinner was again wounded by a musket ball, which passed through both his eyes.

The 28th was the day Pope concentrated, as well as he knew how to do it, his whole army of 50,000 men on Jackson's 22,000, but the modern Cæsar was no match in generalship for our "Stonewall," who was now engaged in the "overt act of war" right between Pope and his capital city, and only a day's march from it. But I shall not attempt any description of the three days' battle of Manassas No. 2, in which the shallow, braggart, persecutor of Virginia women and children—John Pope—was whipped, and, so far as far as fame and character are concerned, personally annihilated—"the deserter desolate." Nor have I any apology for expressing so much of an opinion of him, which, so far as my knowledge goes, is shared by all decent people North and South, by his own soldiers as well as ours; and moreover, the great marauder of hen-roosts, milk-houses and wardrobes is *still living*.

We used to notice one curious difference between the Northern and Southern generals during the war. Their commanding generals of armies and army corps on battle-days kept at their headquarters, long distance from the field, and using their well-appointed staff officers and couriers exclusively in communicating their orders to the troops, while the Southern generals were up among their men, directing and leading their movements, and encouraging them at the critical points.

I am sure that if the Northern soldiers had been thus led and handled, so they could have had the same confidence in their generals the Southern men had, they would have ended the war in less than four years. Everything else being equal, one man is as good as another, but one soldier, having confidence in his commander, is worth ten half-hearted fellows, who have little faith in their general and only see him at review. We did not have the same discipline—in regard to our generals anyhow—that the Northern army had, and ours did not make the same display of "fuss and feathers" with brilliant staff officers, nor require the same flourishing of caps and saluting with arms presented whenever they met us. Ours met spontaneous salutes of cheers right from the hearts of their admiring soldiers, and I have seen Jackson, Ewell and others, do some very hard riding bareheaded, along the columns to escape the noisy homage of their devoted followers.

Any schoolboy would have known that Pope's proper course was to crush Jackson's corps out of existence, and then turn on Longstreet and perform the same service for him—Gen. Lee's disposition of his army having put it in the power of the Federal commander to do this easily; but Gen. Lee knew his man thoroughly, and trusted fully to his blundering incompetency to admit Longstreet to march his corps through Thoroughfare Gap and unite with Jackson at Manassas, which was done by the 29th. True, Gen. Pope defends himself by bringing charges of "delay," "inefficiency," and even disloyalty against Gen. Porter and others; but the rejoinders of these officers backed by clouds of witnesses, are fatal to General Pope's character for generalship and veracity, and the fact remains perfectly clear that he was out-generaled and out-fought by "Stonewall the Great." Gen. Ulysses S. Grant in his last days, after he had taken the time to examine the case against Porter, fully vindicated him and left Pope's reputaion beyond redemption. But the "boys in blue" made a splendid fight; and attacked our position in charge after charge, only to be driven back with slaughter, and when General Early found they had gotten possession of the railroad cut immediately in his front, he promptly aticked them, drove them out and for two hundred yards into the woods. Here occurred a personal matter which afforded me much pleasure in after years, though at the time only done under the promptings of humanity. As we pressed across the railroad bank, where lay numbers of dead and wounded Federals, I inadvertently stepped on the foot of a wounded man, which brought a groan of pain, and I asked his pardon for the accident. After our line halted—which was in a short distance—I returned to the poor fellow, gave him water, and asked if I could do anything for him. He was very grateful, but thought nothing could be done then; however, I asked my captain, Ayrehart, a noble-souled christian gentleman, to assist me, and we moved the man to a more comfortable position under a tree, where Captain Ayrehart, who had considerable knowledge of surgery, dressed his wounds, and I did what I could to make him comfortable, and, after exchanging slips of paper with our names written on them, I rejoined my company, and in the busy scenes then and afterwards being enacted almost forgot the incident.

In 1885 I was canvassing for a book, trying to make a living for a certain "one-legged rebel," and found myself in Jonesboro, Tennessee. In the course of business I called on a Mr. Locke, of that town—but I will give the account as it was published in the Jonesboro *Herald and Tribune* of May 15th, 1885.

"Only a few weeks ago it was telegraphed over the country that Bill Arp, the noted Georgia humorist, had received from Pennsylvania an autograph album that had been taken from his wife's (then his sweetheart) house more than twenty years ago. Last week a much more remarkable incident happened in Jonesboro. On Wednesday, Mr. John S. Robson, of Virginia, and formerly a member of the 52d regiment of that State, in the Confederate service, came here to canvass for the sale of a book he is publishing, giving incidents of the camp and march as he saw them.

"Mr. Robson had but one leg, having contributed the other to his side of the game, in one of the battles of 1864. In the course of the day he met Mr. J. C. Locke, a citizen of Jonesboro. As soon as Mr. Locke observed the missing leg he remarked to Mr. Robson that he (Locke) had also lost a leg in the war, mentioning the engagement, the 2nd battle of Bull Run, August 29th, 1862. Mr. Locke then began to tell of the kind treatment he had received that day from a young Rebel named Robson. 'Why!' exclaimed Mr. Robson, "I am the young Rebel that took care of you that day.' And sure enough he was. A comparison of incidents established the fact beyond a doubt. Mr. Locke was a member of Company E, 100th Pennsylvania (Roundhead) regiment. In the second engagement at Bull Run he was badly wounded in the leg, just as his command was forced to fall back. While stretched upon the field, in the agonies of a wound that was to cost him his leg, he was approached by a boyish-looking rebel, who asked him if he would not like to be moved to a more comfortable place, at the same time offering to have his wounds dressed by his officer, Capt. Ayrhart, who had some knowledge of surgery. The young Rebel advised Locke that if he had anything in his knapsack which he cared to preserve he had better put it h's blouse pocket. This he did, presenting his rebel savior with a razor from a shaving outfit he carried. When the wounded Federal was comfortably fixed, the two soldiers parted, each writing down the other's name. The Rebel was Mr. John S. Robson.

"The two men never met or heard of each other from that day until Wednesday of last week, though they had often thought of one another. Of course the meeting was a happy one, for it was the renewal of an undying friendship, formed in the midst of war's carnage. No doubt, during the rebellion, there occurred many incidents similar to the nobility exhibited by the Virginian to the Pennsylvanian, but it is rare the actors meet, as our two soldiers did, after so many years have intervened."

CHAPTER IX.

I have straggled again but will join the march once more. After Manassas we turned our faces towards the Potomac, and had more hard marching before us, and scant rations again. The roasted corn and green apples had not given out yet, but our wagon trains failed to get up, and we longed for the quantity of good things that were burned up at Manassas. Our march led us into Loudoun county, Virginia, and here we fared better than among the pines and red gullies of Prince William. At our camp near Leesburg, a good story of McLaws' men got out. It seems that when Gen. McLaws' division went into bivouac, hunger had got the better of their morals, and many of them made a raid on a cornfield for rations. The owner called on the General to protect his property, and he ordered guards to surround the field, arrest every man coming out with corn and bring him and his plunder to headquarters. It was not long until the "pirouters" began to appear, under guard, in the presence of the irate commander, and as each one, with his arm load of corn, halted before him, the General opened on him like this: "Where did you get that corn?" and the culprit would begin: "Why, General, I had nothing to eat for three days and I didn't know when the wagons would come"— but there the General stopped him with the order "Put it down there on the ground and go join your command immediately!" This movement, being many times repeated, caused quite a large pile of corn to grow up in front of the General's quarters, and in answer to the savage-toned query—"What are you going to do with that corn?" every one made the same excuse of "hungry," "wagons not come up &c.," and in each case the order was, "throw it down on that pile and go join your command *immediately.*" Finally, one "gray jacket," who had "caught on" to the manner and form of the proceeding, was brought up and accosted fiercely, with the question: "What are you going to do with that corn?" "Why, sir," said the culprit, briskly, "I'm going to throw it down on that pile thar, and go and join my command immejitly, I *am!*" The General broke down, the guards roared, and the cute Reb. slid out "immejitly," but the quartermaster took charge of the corn and issued it to the men, who made it last until the wagons came up with rations.

On the 5th September we crossed the Potomac at White's Ford, and stood on Maryland soil, but it was only a remnant of the "Army of Northern Virginia" that went over. Thousands of our boys had lagged, worn out, bare-footed, sick, hungry, they *could not* keep up, and so, from actual necessity, twenty thousand men of Lee's army staid in Virginia and crept as best they could, to the rendezvous indicated to them by the General for a rallying point—Winchester. We got to Frederick City on the 6th, and behaved ourselves like good boys, while the good people of Maryland treated us very kindly; but there was no doubt about our having struck them at the wrong time or place. We Rebels didn't have *many* songs peculiarly our own. We had no "Yankee Doodle," no "Star Spangled Banner," no "Hail Columbia," no "Tramp, Tramp, The Boys are Marching," no "John Brown's Body Lies a Moldering in the Clay," no "Rally Round the Flag, Boys," like our blue-backed friends over the way. We had our old stand-by, "Dixie"—good yet—and "Bonnie Blue Flag," but we had another—"Maryland, My Maryland"—which up to this time we had sung with a good deal of hope and vim, for this song asserted positively that, "She Breathes, She Burns, She'll Come, She'll Come," etc., but it didn't take "us generals" of the ranks very long to see that there was a mistake about it somewhere, "Some one had blundered," for *she didn't come*," worth a cent; and the people of this portion of Maryland didn't flock to the "Bonnie Blue," in defence of Southern rights quite as unanimously as we had been led to expect—according to the song—but everthing was grand, and the invasion a pleasure trip, so long as we *knew* Major General Pope commanded the "boys in blue."

However, we soon learned that "Little Mac" was again at the head of the army, and then the idea occurred to "us generals" that our Maryland business had better be attended to promptly. We were not much afraid of them, but they might intimidate the Maryland folks, and prevent them, to some extent from joining us; and moreover, while we fully intended to locate our winter quarters on the Susquehanna, we wished to enjoy ourselves a little while in this plentiful country, and get some fat on our bones before breaking up another army for General McClellan.

It is not surprising, I think, that the Maryland folks looked with some doubt and distrust of final success upon the army of rag-tag-and-bobtail which Gen. Lee marched into their midst. These *might* be the gallant soldiers of "Dixie" who had vanquished the great generals of the North in the Valley of Virginia, the swamps of the Chickahominy and on the plains of Manassas, but they didn't *look* like it. Those tattered battle-flags *might* be crowned with the glory of Kernstown, McDowell, Front Royal, Cross Keys, Port Republic, Seven Pines, Cold Harbour and the Seven Days', Cedar Run, Bristoe, Manassas Nos 1 and 2, but it didn't appear to those Maryland eyes. Nor could they see the scalps of Milroy, Shields, Fremont, Banks, McDowell, McClellan, and Pope which swung from the belt of the A. N. V. The appearance of the army didn't justify the faith in those deeds, and notwithstanding the gate was open and the bars down, they wouldn't walk into the Confed racy yet. And, since Maryland wouldn't fall into line with her Southern sisters, we determined to move on to the North, but before doing this Gen. Lee thought it advisable to take Harper's Ferry back into the Confederate States at any rate, and on the 10th September he sent "Stonewall" to attend to that little matter, and we went along.

We marched by Boonsboro to Williamsport, reaching Martinsburg on the 12th, capturing a large quantity of stores from Gen. White at that place, and sending him with his folks to join Gen. Miles in Harper's Ferry so that we could get them all at once. On the 13th we reached Bolivar, and waited until Gens. McLaws and Walker—the first on the Maryland and the second on the Loudoun Heights—answered our signals. The whole United States force at the Ferry was estimated at 11,000, with plenty of cavalry and artillery. On Monday morning, 15th September, "Stonewall," having the bird in hand, closed his fingers on it by opening a concentric fire of artillery from all commanding points on the Federal forts and camps, thus illustrating the opinion expressed by Gen. Jo. Johnston in '61, of Harper's Ferry as a strategic point. At that time the Richmond government desired him to hold the place against Patterson, the Federal general, but Johnston refused, saying that he didn't propose to be "penned in the mouth of a tunnel," but this is exactly the predicament Gen. Miles found himself in, and Gen. White had "brought his ducks to the same market."

About an hour of this cannonading brought a white flag out on the enemy's works, and Harper's Ferry was ours. Gen. Miles was killed at the moment the flag was displayed, and Gen. White made the surrender, which actually included 11,000 prisoners, 13,000 small arms, 73 cannon, 200 wagons, and an immense amount of camp and garrison furniture. As soon as Gen. Jackson knew the enemy had given up the fight he laid down by a log and went to sleep; thoroughly worn out with fatigue and loss of sleep. Gen. A. P. Hill brought Gen. White out to see him, and waking him up, announced: "General, Gen. White, of the United States Army, desires to arrange the terms of surrender." Jackson made a courteous movement with his hand, and went back to sleep. Gen. Hill roused him a second time, and then "Stonewall" said: "General White the surrender must be unconditional, every indulgence can be granted afterwards." That ended it, for he was asleep again, and Hill walked back with White, but when his nap was out he was himself again, and accorded the most generous terms to his captives.

Our next difficulty was of a much more serious nature, for McClellan was mustering his army at Sharpsburg, on the Antietam; and "us generals" freely expressed our unfeigned regret that Major-General J. Pope had been superceded.

We left Harper's Ferry on the 16th, and joined Gen. Lee the same evening, and our commanders, on both sides, were busy arranging for the big battle that was to come off tomorrow, as coolly as farmers getting ready to plant corn. It was no new business to us now — for the novelty was all worn off — but we did wish for our twenty thousand stragglers in Virginia. The ball opened at daylight, on the 17th, and as one old soldier expressed it, "we fought all day, before breakfast, and went on picket all night before supper." "Fighting" Jo. Hooker was immediately in front of Jackson's line, anybody that complained of employment that day was hard to satisfy.

The thing got very hot among the battery boys, after the preliminary skirmishing had cleared the floor for the dance of death; but about sunrise the infantry advanced in heavy force, their batteries moving forward with them and pouring grape and canister among us at close range. This trouble lasted for some time, and then Hooker threw his whole column suddenly against our line, and the firing was heavy and incessant. The object was to turn Gen. Lee's left, but for more than two hours Jackson's men sustained the almost overwhelming assaults of the best troops McClellan had, and he sent heavy reënforcements to Hooker, so that this wing of our army might be driven back and Gen. Lee forced to retreat. More than half of our men were killed or wounded and then, to crown the trouble, our ammunition gave out. Our two division commanders were gone, Gen. Starke killed and Gen. Lawton, of our division, wounded; and every regimental commander in two brigades were killed or wounded.

Gen. Jackson himself gave the order to "retire slowly," which we did, and the movement seemed to inspire "Fighting Jo's" men, and they crowded us hotter than ever, but now Gen. Hood came to our support with his two Texas brigades, and then the fight begun. Up hill and down, through the woods and the corn-fields, over the ploughed land and the clover, the line of fire swept to and fro as one side or the other gained a temporary advantage. Gen. Sum-

100

came to "Fighting Jo's" a
ned that Jackson would have
e did, would decide the batt
l army; but he still hung
a bull-dog, and just at the
ame in the brigades of Semm
of Barksdale's and McLaw
got quickly into line, and
shed everything forward in
ich compelled Hooker's men
und they had gained from us,
ed them from and beyond
a mile. Of course our wh
ng hard all day to prevent
crossing at the various bri
reek, and more than two hu
lering along that line all the t
s report shows that the res
ackson's position was regard
the battle; but Jackson di
and holding his original
ward promptly with Gen. St
nd attempted to turn McCl
ment he was compelled to s
e enemy's batteries so com
passage between their right
at he would not expose his

an once during this battle J
n until they had fired their la
help came to hold the line
ill our cartride-boxes again,
lark. We staid on the batt

day, in line, waiting for Gen. McClellan's boys to come again, but they didn't do it, and at night, on the 18th, crossed the river into Virginia again.

The invasion was ended, and we decided *not* to winter on the Susquehanna, perhaps because it was too far north for us, and we feared the climate would not agree with us, but when Gen. McClellan sent a column over the river at Shepherdstown, on the 20th, to beat up our quarters and keep us from resting, we let A. P. Hill and Gen. "Jubilee" Early go see about it, and when they got there it was very troublesome for awhile, but our boys drove them into the river where a great many were drowned. By their own account one division lost 3,000 killed and drowned. Our loss was 261, and we got 300 prisoners.

Gen. Lee's army lost at Sharpsburg 8,750 men, killed and wounded; Gen. McClellan's army lost 12,469, killed and wounded. What a commentary on war, for it was a drawn battle!

CHAPTER X.

I find that I am consuming too much space in my attempt to keep my story going along, in a consecutive line, with the history of the operations of Jackson's men, for it of necessity, comes into connection with what was done by the whole army, and yet, in following out my original plan, I cannot avoid it. I have also to deal somewhat with the operations of the enemy, for the story of a war with no reference to let old Hamlet himself, if there was no Hamlet! However, the campaigns of 1862 were now about ended, and we spent the gloriously beautiful month of October in our own beloved Valley of the Shenandoah—resting, getting fat and strong, and that was the happiest time we ever spent during the four years. We did very little except camp duty, unless the destruction of all the railroads in our vicinity might be called duty; and "Stonewall" seems to "go for" a railroad like the fellow who killed the splendid Anaconda in the museum because "it was his rule to kill snakes wherever he found them," just because it was his rule to destroy all railroads he could get at; and we demolished the Baltimore and Ohio from Hedgesville to Harper's Ferry; the Winchester and Potamac we swept entirely off the face of the earth; but it never was much of a railroad anyhow, and the Manassas Gap from Strasburg to Piedmont.

"Stonewall" was the grand object of all the sightseers, and much curiosity was evinced by strangers to get a look at him. In Martinsburg, where the ladies crowded around him, he said: "Ladies, this is the first time I was ever surrounded;" but they cut nearly all the buttons off his clothes—stripped his coat entirely—and took from him "his mangy old cap," as Gen. Dick Taylor called it, giving him, instead, a handsome, tall, black hat, but he damaged that as much as he could by turning the brim down all around wearing it so.

In November, when we were marching through Middletown on our way to Fredericksburg, a very old woman, who had a grandson somewhere in the army, hailed the General with the question—"Are you Mr. Jackson?" He told her he was, and asked what she wanted. "I want to see my grandson, I've brought him some clothes and victuals. His name is George Martin, and he belongs to your company!" The General asked her what regiment or brigade he was in, but she couldn't tell, didn't know the name of his captain even, only knew he was in Mr. Jackson's company.

In her distress, she exclaimed—"Why, Mr. Jackson, you certainly know little George Martin! he's been with you in all your battles, and they do say he fit as hard as any of them."

At this, some of the younger members of the staff laughed, but the General turned quickly around, with a blaze in his eye and a thunder cloud on his brow, and that laugh didn't go around—wasn't enough of it; for Jackson looked as if he wanted to find the party who laughed, but the party wasn't laughing then.

Dismounting from his horse, he took the old woman's hand, whose tears were rolling down her face, and in the kindest manner, and simplest words, explained why he didn't know her grandson; but gave her such simple and complete directions as would enable her to find him. We didn't think any the less of "Stonewall," for such foolishness as this of course, but we wanted to hear those Staff fellows laugh some more.

It is hardly necessary to say that "Stonewall" had us at Fredericksburg on time, and on the 13th December he wore a brand-new coat, staff buttons, stars, wreath and all, the same one shown in nearly all the pictures of Jackson I have ever seen, and his men hardly knew him at first. I am not going to tell much about the battle of Fredericksburg. Everybody knows the story of it, from the bombardment and burning of the town by Gen. Burnside's orders to his last crossing, on the night when he took his shivered columns back to Stafford. No doubt but Burnside was fairly beaten and badly broken up, but I am not going to criticise Gen. Lee for allowing him to get away with his army, for I am not a general any more, and the newspaper critics as well as fireside generals have about used up that battle in their discussion of it.

Just here I will introduce a neat bit of satire from Gen. Lee himself, which seems to me to tell it all: In a chat with the Hon. Ben. H. Hill, he said, "We made a great mistake in the beginning of our struggle, and I fear, in spite of all we can do, it will prove a fatal mistake." This was after Gen. Bragg had been removed from command of the army of Tennessee." "What mistake is that, General?" asked Mr. Hill. "Why, sir, in the beginning we appointed all our *worst* generals to command our armies, and all our *best* generals to edit our newspapers. I have done the best I could in the field, and have not succeeded as I could wish. I am willing to yield my place to these *best* generals, and I will do my best for the cause editing a newspaper. Even as poor a soldier as I am can generally discover mistakes after it is all over, but if I could only induce these wise gentlemen who see them so clearly *beforehand* to communicate with me in advance instead of waiting until the evil has come upon us, to let *me* know what *they* knew all the time, it would be far better for the country."

After reading the above I have very little disposition to criticise the actions of Gen. Lee in permitting Burnside's army to lay along the river for nearly two days, and on the night of the 15th December, under the terrible peltings of that awful storm, to get his remnants over the river again, but my memory of the situation at the time checks me, for I can see yet those splendid batteries of great, big, heavy cannon, planted on the heights of Stafford, which would have ground up many a "gray jacket" if our general had put us across the space from Marye's Hill to the Rappahannock, and, knowing that Gen. Burnside was effectually disposed of, I shall let the matter rest.

His was one more added to our list of scalps, but I am told that it was a matter of some uneasiness to General Lee. During the Revolution, so says Irving, General Putnam devised a scheme to raid the British camp in New York town and carry off in a boat no less a personage as prisoner than Sir Henry Clinton himself, the commander-in-chief of their army. This he communicated to Gen. Washington, who sent his aide, Col. Hamilton, to make an inspection, and report as to the feasibility of it. Hamilton performed his task and reported that the thing could be done pretty easily, but recommended that the idea be at once given up. Washington, in surprise, inquired his reason, and Hamilton replied that we knew Sir Henry well and understood him perfectly, but that if he was removed his government might put a man in his place we did not understand, and who might cause us a great deal more trouble than Clinton was doing. Gen. Washington saw the point, and gave orders to let Sir Henry alone.

Gen. Lee said that he didn't like so many changes of commanders of the Army of the Potomac, for they might find a man after awhile who he could not understand, and it would cause trouble for *us*.

The winter of 1862-3 we spent in winter quarters below Moss Neck, about ten miles below Fredericksburg, in barely tolerable comfort; a great deal of the time picketing on the river near Port Royal, with the enemies' pickets just opposite ours, and while I know there was a good deal of deserting going on from their side, I do not think many of our men deserted. We had seen the McDowell-Scott campaign, by way of Manassas, cut short quick—and we had heard and read of the clamor raised by the Northern great Generals, who edited their newspapers, when McClellan took the Peninsula route; many of them insisting on a direct march by the Rappahannock line, and Gen. Burnside had given them that as much as they wanted, and, like the others, had come to grief. Of course we could not tell what their next move would be, but we expected Gen. Lee to put us right in the front whenever the movement was made, and we were very confident of the result; but the inexplicable decree of Divine Providence, which men so often see, yet cannot comprehend, was to be wrought to its full completion; and now we *know* and *realize* the good that was to come, to us out of the gloom and blood and suffering of the afflictive school of civil war.

When spring came, and the roads became passable we began to hear from the boys in blue, on the other side of the Rappahannock; how they had a new commander named—and rightly too—"Fighting Jo

Hooker," and that their army was in better condition, better equipped, if possible, and more fully determined than ever to capture Richmond. Their General had published, to his troops, an order in which he called their attention to the fact that the "Army of the Potamac" was the "finest army on this planet," and that when he put them on the south bank of the Rappahannock, Gen. Lee's army "must either ingloriously fly, or come out from behind their defences and give us battle on our own ground, where certain destruction awaits them." All of which sounded to us a good deal like the programme laid down by Major-General J. Pope, of bombastic memory. After the affair near Harrisonburg, in the Valley, when Col. Sir Percy Wyndham had assumed the special business of "bagging Ashby," and in putting the matter into execution, had, by failure of some part of the arrangement, been snugly bagged himself; one of Ashby's staff, who had been a prisoner at Col. Wyndham's headquarters, and heard his boasting declarations of how he was going to do it, made his escape, rejoined Gen. Ashby and gave him a full account of Sir Percy's actings and doings at the time he started on his "bagging expedition."

Ashby remarked, "it is bad habit in a commander to boast of what he is *going* to do—*especially when doesn't do it.*"

"Fighting Jo" was no such commander as the great Julius C. Pope, however, for he made no war on the women and children of the country, dominated by "the finest army on the planet." He said their situation was bad enough, surrounded as they were by the unavoidable discomforts *naturally* inhering to a state of war, without bringing the *persecuting* power of a military rule to bear upon them ; which sentiment contravens those of General Tecumseh Sherman, when marching through Georgia, after armed resistance to his legion had ceased. His men burned all houses, and destroyed everything they could not carry away, leaving the helpless people utterly destitute ; and, when appealed to on the plea of common humanity, he replied : " War is cruelty and you cannot refine it."

General Hooker commenced to move his army on Monday, April 27th, 1863, and, of course, *we generals* knew all about it immediately, and were wide-awake. We wished much that our " Old Warhorse," General Longstreet, might be with us ; but as he was campaigning in Tennessee, with his veteran corps of the centre, we decided to use what we had, and as the boys said—" give them the best we had in the shop "

We had been through the swamps of the Chickahominy, and ranged in many lands, but the Spottsylvania Wilderness was the worst for a battle ground that had been presented to us up to this time.

Chancellorsville, itself, consisted of a large brick mansion, with ample wings ; and in the days of "Auld Lang Syne" had been used as a tavern for the entertainment of travellers journeying to and from the busy town of Fredericksburg, which rated then as one of the most prominent business centres of the country. That was *all* the town of Chancellorsville, just one house and the outbuildings. In front were extensive fields, but towards the river was the wilderness — dense, impassable for miles, and the most mournful appearing country, especially at night, I had ever seen; and it seemed a good place to die in, where the interminable shadows twined and laced with the mournful, melancholy piping of the whippoorwill; and many a poor fellow did breathe out his life in those gloomy shades, with the weird requiem of "whipporwill" filling all the space of sound about him.

Gen. Lee had to check Hooker's march more by generalship and strategy than by fighting, for he hadn't enough men to meet him in the field. We *soldiers* of Dixie never set up any claim that the army of the Potomac wouldn't fight. That army *would* fight; always fought, and fought hard. They knew they had the advantage of numbers, but they also knew that they were badly handled by their generals; a knowledge that will take the heart out of a soldier quicker than want of ammunition; but they drove right on, and I doubt if any other two commanders than Robert E. Lee and "Stonewall" Jackson, could have taken their sixty-seven thousand men and beaten the one hundred and fifty-nine thousand three hundred troops of "Fighting" Jo Hooker's Army; and Major-General Peck, of the United States Army, gives that as their number.

No finer body of troops could be wished for by a general than Hooker then commanded, nor could it possibly be better equipped—arms of every description, of the latest and most approved styles and kinds; and from the smallest items of clothing, all through the several departments of commissary, quartermaster, ordnance, engineer, medical, nothing that the most lavish expenditure of money, with open ports through which to draw from all the world, was lacking to fit the grand army for this final struggle, as it was then thought to be; for it was pretty generally understood that Lee's army was the backbone of the Confederacy, and that broken, the collapse would be inevitable.

Now back to "Stonewall" again, for the last time, May the 2d, 1863. My regiment was not with Jackson in this fight, it being with that gallant and stubborn old fighting soldier, Gen. Jubal A. Early, who, with his divisions, was at Fredericksburg, holding Sedgwick's force in check at that point. It seems to have been Hooker's design to demonstrate on our right with this army of Gen. Sedgwick, consisting of the 1st, 3d and 6th corps, "Army of the Potomac," inducing Gen. Lee to suppose that the main movement was to be from that direction, and after getting Lee to concentrate at Fredericksburg, he (Gen. Hooker) would move by Kelly's ford, twenty-seven miles above, with the corps of Meade, Howard, Slocum and Couch, cross the Rapidan at Ely's and Germanna fords, turn Lee's left and strike for Gordonsville, thus compelling our army to retreat rapidly on Richmond with Gen. Sedgwick in pursuit; and to render his victory more certain, he sent Gen. Stoneman with ten thousand cavalry on a raid towards Richmond to cut and break up Gen. Lee's railroad communication, and now he announced to his troops that "the Rebel army is the legitimate property of the Army of the Potomac." I suppose everybody has heard schoolboys quarrel, and noticed that just on the edge of a fight over a game of marbles one or the other would pipe up in a high-keyed tone, "You don't know who you're foolin' with!" And that comes pretty near expressing the condition of "Fighting Jo." He didn't know who *he* was fooling with. One of the chief "maxims of Napoleon" was that "the first necessity of a general is to study the character of his opponent," and by this we *know* that Hooker was deficient in generalship, for he should by this time have been sufficiently acquainted with the character of Lee to understand that he could not be cheated by such bungling strategy as was now displayed, and further, when, after he had entrenched himself at Chancellorsville, he learned that "Stonewall" Jackson with a heavy force was in retreat towards Gordonsville, he should have judged that movement by Jackson's character as it had been developed in the war, and he would have understood perfectly what was brewing, for he knew that "retreat without a battle" was no part of the man of Kernstown's pillosophy, and that the soldier who had flanked McClellan out of the Chickahominy and Pope from the Rappahannock, would be quite likely to attempt the same strategy against General Hooker.

A Northern journal of that time, criticising Gen. Hooker's movements in the Chancellorsville campaign, says that "if General Lee had furnished Gen. Hooker with a plan it could not have been more to his liking, for he concentrated first on Hooker and then on Sedgwick, beating both by detail."

A colonel in Hooker's army, who was captured and sent to Richmond after this battle, related that just before Jackson's guns opened on their flank, and while they were talking about his retreat to Gordonsville the surgeon of the colonel's regiment offered to bet a hundred dollars that "Jackson would turn up in the rear." The colonel at once took the bet, firmly believing that such a move was utterly impossible, but it had hardly been closed when firing broke out "in the rear," the "rebel yell" came ringing above the din of battle, "Howard's Flying Dutchmen" broke like horses from the woods, a ragged Confederate demanded the Colonel's surrender, and the surgeon claimed the stakes.

I shall not attempt any account of this battle, for I was on the right, and I know that Gen. Early hampered Gen. Sedgwick—eight thousand of us against twenty-four thousand "boys in blue"—long enough for Gen. Jackson to break up Hooker's lines and for Gen. Lee to drive them over the river and then come down to us, and then Gen. Sedgwick, when the night got dark enough to conceal his movements, retreated, by Banks' ford across the Rappahannock. The battle was over and the victory was ours, but it cost us dear.

Out of our army we had lost in killed, wounded and captured, ten thousand, two hundred and eighty-one—fully one-fourth of what we had, while Hooker's loss was seventeen thousand, one hundred and ninety-seven.

But worse than all we had lost our General and hero, our idol—"Stonewall the Great" was gone from us forever, and the army was in mourning for the victory that had cost us our chief treasure. We had only one "Stonewall," and we could not give him up. We wept for our loss; no soldier thought of pity for Jackson; the soldiers left *behind* were more needy of sympathy. No man said "poor Jackson," or grieved for *him* in sympathy. *He* was the "Great," the "Glorious," the "Triumphant," walking with his God beyond the gates of paradise, but *we* were the bereaved; *our* staff was broken and *our* hearts were sad. Better it was for our General—we believed—to go hence and be at rest; but woe hung over our souls like a cloud, and we could not see the light beyond as we can see it now. Let us put twice two together and see if they make four. Gen. Lee said—not long before his death—that if he could have had Jackson with him at Gettysburg he would have beaten Gen. Meade's army, and Southern independence would have been established; and it is universally conceded that such a result would have surely followed a Southern victory there.

Count that two. Now take Mayor Hewitt, of New York city, in the year of grace, 1888. He says, "it was the South, and not the North, that won in the war between the States." Maybe the old Confederates will not agree with him, but they would if they could realize the immense progress the South has made, to the detriment of the North, since and in consequence of their surrender, and would conclude that the Secessionists, after all, "builded better than they knew." Another broad-minded Northern man says, in a speech at a dinner given by the Southern Society, at New York, on the 22d February, this year:

"I have heard your fight spoken of as the 'Lost Cause.' It has paid you better than any other cause. The South never lost its cause. When everything the South held most dear was swept away, and you were weeping in the valley of the shadow of death, you came to the resurrection which is making the South the garden of this land; which is filling it with wealth won by the labor of freeman and not of slaves. You never knew what you had until you lost the frail crop on which you had planted all your fortunes. God had filled your land with every element of wealth, but it remained undeveloped in the presence of the blight which you neither understood nor realized. Now you have turned your attention to the resources which God has given you, and the "irrepressible conflict" is taking a new shape. It is a conflict between the manufacturing states of the North and the South, and victory is already perching on your banners, and before the lapse of the century the Southern States will far outstrip Pennsylvania and the manufacturing States of the North. It was the North that lost by the outcome of the rebellion, not you; the victory of the North was, in reality, its defeat."

That is the other *two*. Add 'em up!

But we still have our "Stonewall" in memory's heart, as he lived, fought, prayed and died for the independence of our Southern land: died at the precise moment of time and under the exact circumstances best calculated to perpetuate his glory and fame, which today belongs to our common country, North and South, and we, his old veterans, were proud when at the unveiling of his statue in Richmond, on the 27th October, 1875, an almost universal congratulation came to us from our Northern brethren, and such words as these, from the Cincinnati *Enquirer*, were echoed from the Northern press:

"In truth, the character of Stonewall Jackson lifts him above the narrow confines of state or even national limits. His military genius elevates him among the great soldiers of the world, among the select few who belong to the universal history of mankind. He was one of the few born soldiers with whom the conduct of battle was an inspiration, and whose prophetic eye always fixed upon the issue of a struggle as a certainty. Such men are too rare to be confined within the narrow pages of local history, too grand to be repressed by the weight of sectional hostility. They assert their right to universal appreciation and honor. We are rapidly approaching the point when all of us, both North and South, can honor and respect a great name, no matter on which side it came to distinction."

I find I am using too much space for the limits of my little book, and will add but little more, although my idea of the story I have to tell is barely half developed, but I propose to give after awhile the balance of the story, and trust to a generous public to aid the one-legged rebel still further along his life journey.

CHAPTER XI.

My closing chapter of this section of my story of "How a One-Legged Rebel Lives," would not be complete without some personal reminiscence, and I recall a true story of dismay and death which, to my then excited imagination, gave my life upon the altar of the bloody god of war, during the battle of Sharpsburg. In the progress of that all-day, busy battle, the color-bearer of my regiment shot down, and I, with some difficulty, detached the death-grip of his stiffening fingers from the staff and raising the colors carried them forward in their proper place, in the centre of our line.

As we advanced I came upon a canteen which had been dropped by some one, and quickly snatching it up found it was filled, and with the fine instinct which distinguished the average Confederate soldier, concluded that it would be a very laudable scheme to convey that canteen and *contents* to where I was going, and so slinging its strap over my shoulder, I pressed forward, and soon after was dropped by a bullet. I made an examination as soon as I could, and by the quantity of blood flowing from my wounded side was thoroughly satisfied that my wound was mortal and my time short.

I grew rapidly weaker, and after awhile a friend came to me with the intention of assisting me far enough towards the rear to get me in reach of a surgeon, but I was, by this time, too weak to be moved in any other manner than on a stretcher, and my friend proceeded to try his surgical skill in checking the flow of blood. A short examination of the wound brought from him some decidedly emphatic language, and soon he assured me that I wasn't wounded at all, except in the *canteen*, and so it proved, for a bullet had gone through that canteen and its contents, running down my side clear to my shoes, gave me, in connection with the shock, the impression that it was life-blood, when in reality the canteen had been full of molasses. It was long before the boys gave up their chaff about blood and molasses.

Since the war I have had many hard knocks in my efforts to get a living, sometimes succeeding fairly, but often the reverse. Yet still I managed it somehow. One venture, by aid of friends, was successful beyond my most sanguine expectations, and I was in a fair way to achieve a competency—furnishing supplies and running a boarding house on the Chesapeake and Ohio railroad, but in the full tide of success the contractors failed, the hands were left without pay and my last dollar was swept away, but I paid my obligations with one hundred cents to the dollar.

I filled the office of constable for a considerable time, and my experience in that line was mixed with dark and bright color, but the gilding was scarce. I doubt if many country constables, in Virginia, ever achieved great wealth of sheckles.

My best success has been in travelling with books, and I have found kind friends and much sympathy wherever I have gone, many, I know, only taking a book from me to help the one-legged Rebel, and many a hearty reception have I met from the old veterans of the Northern Army. "The bravest are the tenderest; the loving are the daring," and it is easy to read the character of a soldier by his treatment of the maimed victims of the war. True, I have met many veterans who were on the down grade, and had little to help themselves with, but the hearty hand grasp and sympathetic greeting showed the soul within to be of the dauntless host of gallant soldiers of America, who believed that it was blessed to die for the right, and would go at blazing batteries, if necessary.

I have found much kindness among the visitors to and patrons of the various watering places and summer resorts which I have canvassed, and always regardless of section or politics; but I must tell of a gentleman from Michigan, whom I met in Warrenton, Va., a few weeks ago. He was an old soldier from the "Wolverine" State, who had seen much service, but, in bad health, was wintering in Virginia, and hearing of me, made me a call, and we had many pleasant, social and friendly chats. He made himself friends all around, and although much of the conversation was in regard to the war, and that too in the extreme ultra-southern town of Warrenton, the capital of Mosby's Confederacy, and called by the *great* General Pope, the "South Carolina of Virginia." Yet my Michigan friend came out ahead nearly every round. One day a number of us, he among the rest, were discussing the war and fighting our battles over again, when "Michigan" remarked that he had killed a Rebel in the Valley, at the given date, then under discussion. This brought out a somewhat indignant remark from a young man in the party who demanded the particulars. "Well, Sir," said 'Michigan,' "I was over in the Shenandoah Valley with Sheridan, in '64, and I did the killing in one of our battles with General Early. It was on a very hot, dry day in August, and my regiment was trying to hold a ridge in an open field about a quarter of a mile in front of a woods. The Rebels were pressing us hotly; which, together with the weather and want of water, made our situation very distressing, and when they finally advanced upon us with fixed bayonets, we jumped up and made for the woods. A Rebel soldier, who appeared to me to be about nine feet high, with a gun and bayonet the full length of a fence rail, was about twenty yards from me when I started from the ridge, and on my rapid retreat to the woods I could hear his feet pounding the ground behind me, and apparently getting closer to me. I put on all the steam my boiler would carry, for I particularly didn't fancy the contact with that enormous bayonet, which the Rebel evidently intended to use on me, and I fairly flew. Pretty soon I noticed that his foot-falls were growing more indistinct, and with hope renewed I glanced back at him. That glance revealed to me my opportunity, for overcome with the heat and rapid locomotion, which my speed made it necessary for him to use, he was just in the act of falling to the ground, and I then realized for the first time that I had killed a Rebel. He dropped stone-dead, and I reached the timber in safety. My comrades said the man ran himself to death, trying to catch me, but I shall always contend that I killed him with that last spurt."

I myself have cause to remember campaigning in the Valley in 1864, for it was at the battle of Cedar Creek, on the 19th of October, that I received the wound which made me a one-legged Rebel. At this time I was acting as a courier for General John Pegram, commanding Early's old division, and this battle, sometimes called Belle Grove, was one of the most singular of the war. General Early planned it in order to prevent Gen. Sheridan from sending troops to Grant at Petersburg, and because of Sheridan's enormous superiority in numbers, he was compelled to operate by a surprise flank movement, which in conception and execution was equal to the most brilliant of Stonewall Jackson's pieces of strategy, and was completely successful in the early part of it, our boys gallantly driving three corps of the enemy (the 6th, 8th and 19th) clear out of their camps, capturing fifteen hundred prisoners and eighteen pieces of artillery. The surprise was complete, and the Yankee boys fled in panic along the Valley pike, with General Early pressing them with their own artillery, but our soldiers failed to stick to their colors, and so many of them left their ranks to plunder the rich stores of the captured camps that the enemy, under the gallant General Wright, had the opportunity to rally in front of Middletown, and by eleven o'clock had brought up enough troops to move on us, and then these stragglers and plunderers of ours came to grief.

Wright's men recovered their camps, and their cavalry pursued our men so closely that they were forced to retreat to Strasburg. All the success of the morning had been lost, and for the first time in the whole war a victory almost won had been thrown away by the misconduct of Southern solders. Owing to the breaking down of a brigade at the very narrow part of the road between Strasburg and Fisher's Hill, just above Strasburg, where there was no other passway, all the artillery, ordnance wagons and ambulances which had not passed that point were captured by a small body of Sheridan's cavalry, our force which would have defended and brought them out having been broken when the gallant Ramseur was killed.

This battle ended my campaigning for that war, after passing through the mill, and after receiving my severe wound that afterwards caused the amputation of my right leg.

The boys in the hospitals had their jokes on the surgeons, and this propensity for joking and fun among our soldiers was worth almost as much as medicine. One case they reported was that of a man brought in, dangerously wounded in three places. After the examination by the surgeon, an assistant asked: "Doctor, is the man badly hurt?" "Yes," said the surgeon, "two of the wounds are mortal, but the third can be cured provided the man is kept perfectly quiet for six weeks."

CHAPTER XII.

As a matter of interest to the old veterans of the war, into whose hands this little book may fall, I append here the rosters of the two great armies which contended at Gettysburg, that being generally conceded to be the decisive battle.

We understand that at the opening of the campaign the two armies were more evenly matched, as to numbers, than at any other period of the war, and from the best obtainable information that General Hooker had a force of eighty thousand infantry divided into seven corps. So he himself wrote to President Lincoln, and proudly called it "the finest army on the planet."

General Lee's army, by the last of May, had seventy thousand infantry—in three corps—and ten thousand cavalry, and, as Gen. Longstreet expressed it, "was in a condition to undertake anything."

The actual force of Gen. Lee's army at Gettysburg after making details to guard the lines of communication, &c., was about sixty-two thousand men; and Gen. Meade, by the aid of re-enforcements, brought forward by stress of the invasion, numbered about one hundred and twelve thousand.

Organization of the Army of Northern Virginia, June 1st, 1863—General Robert E. Lee, commanding:

STAFF.

Colonel W. H. Taylor, Adjutant-General.
" C. S. Venable, A. D. C.
" Charles Marshall, A. D. C.
" James L. Corley, Chief Quartermaster.
" R. G. Cole, Chief Commissary.
" B. G. Baldwin, Chief of Ordnance.
" H. E. Peyton, Assistant Inspector-General.
General W. N. Pendleton, Chief of Artillery.
Doctor L. Guild, Medical Director.
Colonel W. Porcher Smith, Chief Engineer.
Major H. E. Young, Assistant Adjutant-General.
" G. B. Cook, Assistant Inspector-General.

FIRST CORPS.

Lieutenant-General James Longstreet, commanding.

M'LAWS' DIVISION.

Major-General L. McLaws, commanding.
Kershaw's Brigade—Brigadier-General J. B. Kershaw, commanding; 15th South Carolina regiment, Col. W. D. DeSaussure; 8th South Carolina, Col. J. W. Memminger; 2d South Carolina, Col. John D. Kennedy; 3d South Carolina, Col. James D. Nance; 7th South Carolina, Col. D. Wyatt Aiken; 3d (James) Battalion, South Carolina Infantry, Lieut-Col. R. C. Rice.
Benning's Brigade—Brigadier-General H. L. Benning, commanding: 50th Georgia regiment, Col. W. R. Manning; 51st Georgia regiment, Col. W. M. Slaughter; 53d Georgia regiment, Col. James P. Simms; 10th Georgia regiment, Lieut.-Col. John B. Weems.
Barksdale's Brigade—Brigadier-General William Barksdale, commanding; 13th Mississippi regiment, Col. J. W. Car-

ter; 17th Mississippi regiment, Col. W. D. Holder; 18th Mississippi regiment, Col. Thomas M. Griffin; 21st Mississippi regiment, Col. B. G. Humphreys.

Wofford's Brigade—Brigadier-General W. T. Wofford, commanding; 18th Georgia regiment, Major E. Griffs; Phillips' Georgia Legion, Col. W. M. Phillips; 24th Georgia regiment, Col. Robert McMillan; 16th Georgia regiment, Col. Goode Bryan; Cobb's Georgia Legion, Lieut-Col. L. D. Glewn.

PICKETT'S DIVISION.

Major-General George E. Pickett, commanding.

Garnett's Brigade—Brigadier-General R. B. Garnett, commanding; 8th Virginia regiment, Col. Eppa Hunton; 18th Virginia regiment, Col. R. E. Withers; 19th Va. regiment, Col. Henry Gantt; 28th Va. regiment, Col. R. C. Allen; 56th Va. regiment, Col. W. D. Stuart.

Armistead's Brigade—Brigadier-General L. A. Armistead, commanding; 9th Virginia regiment, Lieut.-Col. J. S. Gilliam; 14th Virginia regiment, Col. J. G. Hodges; 38th Virginia regiment, Col. E. C. Edmonds; 53d Virginia regiment, Col. John Grammar; 57th Virginia regiment, Col. J. B. Magruder.

Kemper's Brigade—Brigadier-General J. L. Kemper, commanding; 1st Virginia regiment, Col. Lewis B. Williams, Jr.; 3d Virginia regiment, Col. Joseph Mayo, Jr.; 7th Virginia regiment, Col. W. T. Patton; 11th Virginia regiment, Col. David Funsten; 24th Virginia regiment, Col. W. R. Terry.

Corse's Brigade—Brigadier-General M. D. Corse, commanding; 15th Virginia regiment, Col. T. P. August; 17th Virginia regiment, Col. Morton Marye; 30th Virginia regiment, Col. A. T. Harrison; 32d Virginia regiment, Col. E. B. Montague (this brigade was not at Gettysburg, having been left at Hanover Junction).

HOOD'S DIVISION.

Major-General, John B. Hood.

Robertson's Brigade—Brigadier-General J. B. Robertson, commanding; 1st Texas regiment, Col. A. T. Rainey; 4th Texas regiment, Col. J. C. G. Key; 5th Texas regiment, Colonel R. M. Powell; 3d Arkansas regiment, Colonel Van H. Manning.

Laws' Brigade—Brigadier-General E. M. Laws, commanding. 4th Alabama regiment, Colonel P. A. Bowles; 44th Alabama regiment, Col. W. H. Perry; 15th Aabama regiment,

Colonel James Canty; 47th Alabama regiment, Colonel J. W. Jackson; 48th Alabama regiment, Colonel J. F. Shepherd.

Anderson's Brigade—Brigadier-General G. T. Anderson commanding; 10th Georgia battalion, Major J. E. Rylander; 7th Georgia regiment, Col. W. M. White; 8th Georgia regiment, Lieut.-Colonel J. R. Towers; 9th Georgia regiment, Colonel B. F. Beck; 11th Georgia regiment, Colonel F. H. Little.

Jenkins' Brigade—Brigadier-General M. Jenkins, commanding; 2d South Carolina Rifles, Col. Thomas Thompson; 1st South Carolina regiment, Lieut.-Col. David Livingstone; 5th South Carolina regiment, Col. A. Coward; 6th South Carolina regiment, Col. John Bratton; Hampton's Legion, Colonel M. W. Gary.

ARTILLERY OF THE FIRST CORPS.

Colonel J. B. Walton, commanding.
Battalion—Col. H. C. Cabell; Major Hamilton.
Batteries—McCarty's, Manly's, Carlton's, Frazer's.
Battalion—Major Henry.
Batteries—Bachman's, Reilly's, Latham's, Gordon's.
Battalion—Major Dearing, Major Reed.
Batteries—Macon's, Blount's, Stribbling's, Caskie's.
Battalion—Col. E. P. Alexander, Major Huger.
Batteries—Jordon's, Rhett's, Moody's, Parker's, Taylor's.
Battalion—Major Eshleman.
Batteries—Squire's, Miller's, Richardson's, Norcom's.
Total number of guns—artillery First Corps—83.

SECOND CORPS.

Lieutenant-General Richard S. Ewell.

EARLY'S DIVISION.

Major-General Jubal A. Early, commanding.

Hays' Brigade—Brigadier-General Harry S. Hays, commanding; 5th Louisiana regiment, Col. Henry Forno; 6th Louisiana regiment, Col. Wm. Monaghan; 7th Louisiana regiment, Col. D. B. Penn; 8th Louisiana regiment, Col. Henry B. Kelly; 9th La. regiment, Col. A. L. Stafford.

Gordon's Brigade—Brigadier-General J. B. Gordon, commanding; 13th Georgia, Col. J. M. Smith; 26th Georgia, Col. E. N. Atkinson; 31st Georgia, Col. C. A. Evans; 38th Georgia, Major J. D. Matthews, 60th Georgia, Col. W. H Stiles; 61st Georgia, Col. J. H. Lamar.

Smith's Brigade—Brigadier-General William Smith commanding; 13th Virginia regiment, Col. J. E. B. Terrell

31st Virginia, Col. J. S. Hoffman, 49th Virginia, Colonel Gibson ; 52d Virginia, Colonel Skinner ; 58th Virginia, Col. F. H. Board—13th Virginia was left in Winchester to guard the stores captured from Milroy, and 58th Virginia was left in Staunton to guard prisoners captured from Milroy.

Hoke's Brigade—Colonel J. B. Avery, commanding, (Gen. R. F. Hoke being absent wounded); 5th North Carolina regiment, Col. J. E. Avery ; 21st North Carolina, Col. W. W. Kirkland ; 54th North Carolina, Col. J. C. T. McDonald ; 57th North Carolina, Col. A. C. Godwin ; 1st North Carolina battalion, Major R. H. Wharton.

RODES' DIVISION.

Major-General R. E. Rodes.

Daniel's Brigade—Brigadier-General Junius Daniel, commanding ; 32d North Carolina regiment, Col. E. C. Bravale ; 43d North Carolina, Col. Thomas S. Keenan ; 45th North Carolina, Lieut-Col. Samuel H. Boyd, 53d North Carolina, Col. W. A. Owens ; 2d North Carolina Battalion, Lieut-Col. H. S. Andrews.

Doles' Brigade—Brigadier General George Doles, commanding ; 4th Georgia, Lieut-Col. D. R. E. Winn ; 12th Georgia, Col. Edward Willis ; 21st Georgia, Col. John T. Mercer ; 44th Georgia, Col. S. P. Lumpkin.

Ramseur's Brigade—Brigadier-General S. D. Ramseur, commanding ; 2d North Carolina regiment, Major E. W. Hurt ; 4th North Carolina, Col. Bryan Grimes ; 14th North Carolina, Col. R. T. Bennett ; 30th North Carolina, Col. F. M. Parker.

Iverson's Brigade—Brigadier-General Alfred Iverson, commanding ; 5th North Carolina regiment, Capt. S. B. West ; 12th North Carolina, Lieut-Col. W. S. Davis ; 20th North Carolina, Lieut-Col. N. Slough ; 23d North Carolina, Col. D. H. Christie.

Rodes' Brigade—Col. E. A. Oneal, commanding ; 3d Alabama regiment, Col. C. A. Battle ; 5th Alabama, Col. J. M. Hall ; 6th Alabama, Col. J. N. Lightfoot ; 12th Alabama, Col. S. B. Pickens ; 26th Alabama, Lieut-Col. J. C. Goodgame.

JOHNSON'S DIVISION.

Major-General Edward Johnson.

Stuart's Brigade—Brigadier-General Geo. H. Stuart, commanding ; 10th Virginia regiment, Col. E. T. H. Warren ; 23d Virginia, Col. A. G. Taliaferro, 27th Virginia, Col. T.

V. Williams; 1st North Carolina regiment, Col. J. A. McDowell; 3d North Carolina, Lieut-Col. Thurston.
Stonewall Brigade—Brig.-Gen. James A. Walker, commanding; 2d Virginia regiment, Col. J. G. A. Nadensbousch; 4th Virginia, Col. Chas. A. Ronald; 5th Virginia, Col. J. H. S. Funk; 27th Virginia, Col. J. K. Edmondson; 33d Virginia. Col. F. M. Holliday.
Jones' Brigade—Brig.-Gen. John M. Jones, commanding; 21st Virginia regiment, Captain Moseley; 42d Virginia, Lieut.-Col. Withers; 44th Virginia, Captain Buckner; 48th Virginia, Col. T. S. Garnett; 50th Virginia, Col. Vandevauter.
Nicholl's Brigade—Col. J. M. Williams, commanding (Gen. F. T. Nicholls wounded); 1st Louisiana regiment, Colonel William R. Shivers; 2d Louisiana regiment, Col. J. M. Williams; 10th Louisiana regiment, Col. E. Waggaman; 14th Louisiana regiment, Col. Z. York; 15th Louisiana regiment, Col. Edward Pendleton.

ARTILLERY OF THE SECOND CORPS.

Colonel S. Crutchfield, commanding.
Battalion—Lieut.-Col. Thomas H. Carter; Major Carter M. Braxton.
Batteries—Captain Page's, Fry's, Carter's, Reese's.
Battalion—Lieut.-Col. H. P. Jones, Major Brockenborough.
Batteries—Carrington's, Garber's, Thompson's, Tanner's.
Battalion—Lieut.-Col. S. Andrews, Major Lattimer.
Batteries—Brown's, Dermot's, Carpenter's, Raines's.
Battalion—Lieut.-Col. Nelson, Major Page.
Batteries—Kirkpatrick's, Massie's, Milledge's.
Battalion—Col. J. T. Brown, Major Hardaway.
Batteries—Dance's, Watson's, Smith's, Huff's, Graham's.
Total number of guns, artillery Second Corps, 82.

THIRD CORPS.

Lieutenant-General A. P. Hill, commanding.

ANDERSON'S DIVISION.

Major-General R. H. Anderson.
Wilcox's Brigade—Briadier-General Cadmus M. Wilcox; 8th Alabama regiment, Col. T. L. Royster; 9th Alabama, Col. S. Henry; 10th Alabama, Col. W. H. Forney; 11th Alabama, Col. J. C. C. Saunders; 14th Alabama, Col. L. P. Pinkhard.
Mahone's Brigade—Brig.-Gen. Wm. Mahone; 6th Virginia regiment, Col. G. T. Rogers; 12th Virginia, Col. D. A.

Weisiger; 16th Virginia, Lieut.-Col. Joseph H. Ham; 41st Virginia, Col. W. A. Parham; 61st Virginia, Col. V. D. Groner.
Posey's Brigade—Brigadier-General Carnot Posey; 46th Mississippi, Col. Joseph Payne; 16th Mississippi, Col. S. E. Baker; 19th Mississippi, Col. John Mullins; 12th Mississippi, Col. W. H. Taylor.
Wright's Brigade — Brigadier-General A. R. Wright; 2d Georgia battalion, Major G. W. Ross; 3d Georgia regiment, Col. E. J. Walker; 22d Georgia regiment, Col. R. H. Jones; 48th Georgia regiment, Col. Wm. Gibson.
Perry's Brigade—Brigadier-General E. A. Perry; 2d Florida regiment, Lieut.-Col. S. G. Pyles; 5th Florida, Col. J. C. Hately; 8th Florida, Col. David Long.

HETH'S DIVISION.

First Brigade—Brigadier-General Pettigrew; 42d, 11th, 26th, 44th, 47th, 52d, 17th North Carolina regiments.
Second Brigade—Brigadier-General Field, 40th, 55th, 47th Virginia regiments.
Third Brigade — Brigadier-General Archer; 1st, 7th, 14th Tennessee regiments, 13th Alabama regiment.
Fourth Brigade—Brigadier-General Cook; 15th, 27th, 46th 48th North Carolina regiments.
Fifth Brigade—Brigadier-General Davis; 2d, 11th and 42d Mississippi, and 55th North Carolina regiments.

MAJOR-GENERAL PENDER'S DIVISION.

First Brigade—Brigadier-General McGowan; 1st, 12th, 13th, and 14th South Carolina regiments.
Second Brigade—Brigadier-General Lane; 7th, 18th, 28th, 33d, and 37th Georgia regiments.
Third Brigade—Brigadier-General Thomas; 14th, 35th, 45th, and 49th Georgia regiments.
Fourth Brigade—Pender's old brigade; 13th, 16th, 22d, 34th, and 38th North Carolina regiments.

ARTILLERY OF THE THIRD CORPS.

Colonel R. Lindsay Walker, commanding.
Battalion—Major D. G. McIntosh, Major W. F. Poague.
Batteries—Hurt's, Rice's, Luck's, Johnson's.
Battalion—Lieut-Colonel Garnett, Major Richardson.
Batteries—Lewis's, Maurin's, Moore's, Grandy's.
Battalion—Major Cutshaw.
Batteries—Wyatt's, Woolfolk's, Brooke's.
Battalion—Major Willie P. Pegram.

Batteries—Brunson's, Davidson's, Crenshaw's, Magraw's, Marye's.
Battalion—Lieut-Colonel Cutts. Major Lane.
Batteries—Wingfield's, Ross's, Patterson's.
  Total number of guns, Artillery of Third Corps, 83.
  Total number of guns, Army Northern Virginia, 248.

CAVALRY CORPS, A. N. V.

Major-General J. E. B. Stuart.
Hampton's Brigade—Brigadier-General Wade Hampton, commanding.
Fitz. Lee's Brigade—Brigadier-General Fitzhugh Lee, commanding.
W. H. F. Lee's Brigade—Colonel Chambliss, commanding.
Robertson's Brigade—Brigadier-General B. H. Robertson, commanding.
Jone's Brigade—Brigadier-Gen. W. E. Jones, commanding.
Imboden's Brigade—Brigadier-General J. D. Imboden, commanding.
Jenkens' Brigade—Brigadier-General A. G. Jenkens, commanding.
White's Battalion—Lieut.-Col. E. V. White, commanding.
Baker's Brigade—

Roster of the Federal Army, engaged in the battle of Gettysburg, Wednesday, Thursday, and Friday, July 1st, 2d, and 3d, 1863,—Major-General Geo. G. Meade, commanding.

STAFF:

Major-General Daniel Butterfield, Chief of Staff.
Brigadier-General M. R. Patrick, Provost Marshal-General.
  "   Seth Williams, Adjutant-General.
  "   Edmund Schriver, Inspector-General.
  "   Rufus Ingalls, Quartermaster-General.
Col. Henry F. Clarke, Chief Commissary of Subsistence.
Major Jonathon Letterman, Surgeon, Chief of Medical Department.
Brigadier-General G. K. Warren, Chief Engineer.
Major G. W. Flagler, Chief of Ordnance.
Major-General Alfred Pleasanton, Chief of Cavalry.
Brigadier-General Henry J. Hunt, Chief of Artillery.
Captain L. B. Norton, Chief Signal Officer.

Major-General John F. Reynolds, commanding the First, Third, and Eleventh Corps, on July 1st.
Major-General Henry W. Slocum, commanding the Right Wing, on July 2d, and 3d.
Major-General Winfield S. Hancock, commanding the Left Centre, on July 2d, and 3d.

FIRST CORPS.

Major-General John F. Reynolds, Permanent Commander.
Major-General Abner Doubleday, commanding on July 1st.
Major-General John Newton, commanding on July 2d, and 3d.

FIRST DIVISION.

Brigadier-General James S. Wadsworth, commanding.
First Brigade—Brigadier-General Solomon Meredith, wounded and succeeded by Col. H. A. Morrow; also wounded and succeeded by Col. W. W. Robinson; 2d Wisconsin, Col. Lucius Fairchild; 6th Wisconsin, Col. R. R. Dawes; 7th Wisconsin, Col. W. W. Robinson; 24th Michigan, Col. H. A. Morrow; 19th Indiana, Col. Samuel Williams.
Second Brigade—Brigadier-General Lysander Cutler, commanding; 7th Indiana, Major Ira G. Grover; 56th Pennsylvania, Col. J. W. Hoffman; 76th New York, Major A. J. Grover; 95th New York, Col. Geo. H. Biddle; 147th New York, Lieut-Col. F. C. Miller; 14th Brooklyn, Col. E. B. Fowler.

SECOND DIVISION.

Brigadier-General John C. Robinson, commanding.
First Brigade—Brigadier-General Gabriel R. Paul, commanding; 16th Maine, Col. Chas. W. Tilden; 13th Massachusetts, Col. S. H. Leonard; 94th New York, Col. A. R Root; 104th New York, Col. Gilbert G. Prey; 107th Pennsylvania, Col. T. F. McCoy; 11th Pennsylvania, Col. R. S. Coulter.

THIRD DIVISION.

Major-General Abner Doubleday, commanding.
First Brigade—Brigadier-General Thomas A. Rowley, commanding; 121st Pennsylvania, Col. Chapman Biddle; 142d Pennsylvania, Col. Robt. P. Cummings; 151st Pennsylvania, Lieut-Col. George F. McFarland; 20th New York, S. M., Col. Theodore B. Gates.
Second Brigade—Col. Roy Stone, commanding; 143d Pennsylvania, Col. Edmund L. Dana; 149th Pennsylvania, Lieut-Col. Walton Dwight; 150th Pennsylvania, Col. Langhorne Wistar.

Third Brigade—Brigadier-General George J. Stannard; 12th Vermont, Col. Asa P. Blount; 13th Vermont, Col. Francis V. Randall; 14th Vermont, Col. W. T. Nichols; 15th Vermont, Col. Redfield Proctor; 16th Vermont, Col. W. G. Veazey.

Artillery Brigade—Col. Chas. S. Wainwright; 2d Maine, Capt. James A. Hall; 5th Maine. Capt. G. T. Stevens; Battery B, 1st Pennsylvania, Capt. J. H. Cooper; Battery B, 4th United States, Lieut. James Stewart; Battery L, 1st New York, Capt. J. A. Reynolds.

SECOND CORPS.

Major-General Winfield S. Hancock, commanding.

FIRST DIVISION.

Brigadier-General John C. Caldwell.

First Brigade—Col. Edward E. Cross, commanding; 5th New Hampshire, Col. E. E. Cross; 61st New York, Lieut-Col. Oscar K. Broady; 81st Pennsylvania, Col. H. Boyd McKeen; 148th Pennsylvania: Lieut-Col. Robert McFarland.

Second Brigade—Colonel Patrick Kelly, commanding; 28th Massachusetts, Col. Richard Byrnes; 63d New York, Lieut-Col. R. C. Bentley; 69th New York, Capt. Maroney; 88th New York, Col. Patrick Kelley; 116th Pennsylvania, Major St. C. A. Mulholland.

Third Brigade—Brigadier-General S. K. Zook; 52d New York, Lieut-Col. Charles G. Freudenberg; 57th New York, Lieut-Col. A. B. Chapman; 66th New York, Col. Orlando W. Morris; 140th Pennsylvania, Col. Richard P. Roberts.

Fourth Brigade—Col. John R. Brooke, commanding; 27th Connecticut, Lieut-Col. Henry C. Merwin; 64th New York, Col. Daniel G. Bingham; 53d Pennsylvania, Lieut-Col. Richard McMichael; 145th Pennsylvania, Col. H. L. Brown; 2d Delaware, Col. William P. Bailey.

SECOND DIVISION.

Brigadier-General John Gibbon, commander.

First Brigade—Brigadier-General William Harrow; 19th Maine, Col. F. E. Heath; 15th Massachusetts, Col. Geo. H. Ward; 82d New York, Col. Henry W. Huston; 1st Minnesota, Col. William Colvil.

Second Brigade—Brigadier-General Alexander S. Webb; 69th Pennsylvania, Col. Dennis O. Kane; 71st Pennsylvania, Lieut-Col. R. Penn Smith; 72d Pennsylvania, Col. D. W. C. Baxter; 106th Pennsylvania, Lieut-Col. Theodore Hesser.

Third Brigade—Col. Norman J. Hall, commanding; 19th Massachusetts, Col. Arthur P. Devereux; 20th Massachusetts, Col. Paul J. Revere; 42d New York, Col J. E. Mallon; 59th New York, Lieut-Col. Max A. Thoman; 7th Michigan, Col. N. J. Hall. Unattached—The Andrew Sharpshooters.

THIRD DIVISION.

Brigadier-General Alexander Hays, commanding.
First Brigade—Col. Samuel S. Carroll, commanding; 4th Ohio, Lieut-Col. James H. Godman; 8th Ohio, Lieut-Col. Franklin Sawyer; 14th Indiana, Col. John Coons; 7th West Virginia, Col. Joseph Snyder.
Second Brigade—Col. Thomas A. Smyth, commanding; 14th Connecticut, Major J. T. Ellis; 10th New York, Major J. F. Hopper; 108th New York, Col. C. J. Powers; 12th New Jersey, Major J. T. Hill; 1st Delaware, Lieut-Col. Edward P. Harris.
Third Brigade—Col. George L. Willard, commanding; 39th New York, Lieut-Col. James G. Hughes; 111th New York, Col. Clinton D. McDougall; 125th New York, Lieut-Col. L. Crandall; 126th New York, Col. E. Sherrell.
Artillery Brigade—Capt. J. G. Hazzard, commanding; Battery B, 1st New York, Capt. James McK. Rorty; Battery B, 1st Rhode Island, Lieut. T. Frederick Brown; Battery A, 1st Rhode Island, Lieut. Wm. A. Arnold; Battery I, 1st United States, Lieut. G. A. Woodruff; Battery A, 4th United States, Lieut. A. H. Cushing.
Cavalry Squadron—Capt. Riley Johnson, commanding; companies D and K, 6th New York.

THIRD CORPS.

Major-General Daniel E. Sickles.

FIRST DIVISION.

Major-General David B. Birney.
First Brigade—Brigadier-General C. K. Graham; 57th Pennsylvania, Col. Peter Sides; 63d Pennsylvania, Lieut-Col. John A. Danks; 68th Pennsylvania, Col. A. H. Tippin; 105th Pennsylvania, Col. Calvin A. Craig; 114th Pennsylvania, Lieut-Col. Fred. K. Cavada; 141st Pennsylvania, Col. H. J. Madill. (Note—The 2d New Hampshire, 3d Maine, 7th and 8th New Jersey, also formed part of Graham line on the 2d.)
Second Brigade—Brigadier-General J. H. H. Ward; 1st United States Sharpshooters, Col. H. Berdan; 4th Maine, Col. Elijah Walker; 2d United States Sharpshooters, Major H. H. Stoughton; 3d Maine, Col. M. B. Lakeman; 20th Indiana, Col. John Wheeler;

99th Pennsylvania, Major John W. Moore; 86th New York, Lieut-Col. Benjamin Higgins; 124th New York, Col. A. Van Horn Ellis.
Third Brigade—Col. Philip R. De Trobriand, commanding; 3d Michigan, Col. Byron R. Pierce; 5th Michigan, Lieut-Col. John Pulford; 40th New York. Col. Thomas W. Eagan; 17th Maine, Lieut-Col. Charles B. Merrill; 110th Pennsylvania, Lieut-Col. D. M. Jones.

SECOND DIVISION.

Brigadier-General Andrew A. Humphreys.
First Brigade—Brigadier-General Joseph B. Carr; 1st Massachusetts, Col. N. B. McLaughlin; 11th Massachusetts, Lieut-Col. Porter D. Tripp; 16th Massachusetts, Lieut-Col. Waldo Merriam; 26th Pennsylvania, Captain Geo.W. Tomlinson; 11th New Jersey, Col. Robert McAllister; 84th Pennsylvania (not engaged), Lieut-Col. Milton Opp; 12th New Hampshire, Capt. J. F. Langley.
Second Brigade—Col. William R. Brewster, commanding; 70th New York (1st Excelsior) Major Daniel Mahen; 71st New York (2nd Excelsior) Col. Henry L. Potter; 72nd New York (3d Excelsior) Col. William O. Stevens; 73d New York (4th Excelsior) Major M. W. Burns, 74th New York (5th Excelsior) Lieut-Col. Thomas Holt; 120th New York, Lieut-Col. Cornelius D. Westbrook.
Third Brigade—Col. George C. Burling, commanding; 5th New Jersey, Col. W. J. Sewell; 6th New Jersey, Lieut-Col. S. R. Gilkyson, 7th New Jersey, Col. L. R. Francine; 8th New Jersey, Col. John Ramsey; 115th Pennsylvania, Lieut-Col. J. P. Dunne; 2d New Hampshire, Col. E. L. Bailey.
Artillery Brigade — Captain George E. Randolph, commanding; Battery E, 1st Rhode Island, Lieut. J. K. Bucklyn; Battery B, 1st New Jersey, Capt. A. J. Clark; Battery D, 1st New Jersey, Capt. George T. Woodbury; Battery K, 4th United States, Lieut. F. W. Seeley; Battery D, 1st New York, Capt. George B Winslow; 4th New York, Capt. James E. Smith.

FIFTH CORPS.

Major-General George Sykes, commanding.

FIRST DIVISION.

Brigadier-General James Barnes, commanding.
First Brigade—Col. W. S. Tilton, commanding. 18th Massachusetts, Col. Joseph Hayes; 22d Massachusetts, Lieut.-Col. Thomas Sherman, Jr.; 118th Pennsylvania, Col. Charles M. Prevost; 1st Michigan, Col. Ira C. Abbott.
Second Brigade—Col. J. B. Sweitzer, commanding; 9th Massachu

setts, Col. Patrick R. Guiney; 32d Massachusetts, Col. George L. Prescott; 4th Michigan, Col. Hamson H. Jeffords; 62d Pennsylvania, Lieut.-Col. James C. Hill.

Third Brigade—Col. Strong Vincent, commanding; 20th Maine, Col. Joshua L. Chamberlain; 44th New York, Col. James C. Rice; 83d Pennsylvania, Major Wm. H. Lamont; 16th Michigan, Lieut.-Col. N. E. Welch.

SECOND DIVISION.

Brigadier-General Romayn B. Ayres, commanding.

First Brigade—Col. Hannibal Day, 6th U. S. Infantry, commanding; 3d United States Infantry, Capt. H. W. Freedley; 4th United States Infantry, Capt. J. W. Adams; 6th United States Infantry, Capt. Levi C. Bootes; 12th United States Infantry, Capt. Thomas S. Dunn; 14th United States Infantry, Major G. R. Giddings.

Second Brigade—Col. Sidney Burbank, 2d U. S. Infantry, commanding; 2d United States Infantry, Major A. T. Lee; 7th United States Infantry, Capt. D. P. Hancock; 10th United States Infantry, Capt. William Clinton; 11th United States Infantry, Maj. DeL. Floyd Jones; 17th United States Infantry, Lieut.-Col. Durrell Green.

Third Brigade—Brigadier-General S. H. Weed; 140th New York, Col. Patrick H. O'Rorcke; 146th New York, Col. Kenner Garrard; 91st Pennsylvania, Lieut.-Col. J. H. Sinex; 155th Pennsylvania, Lieut-Col. John H. Cain.

THIRD DIVISION.

Brigadier General S. Wiley Crawford.

First Brigade—Col. William McCandless commanding; 1st Pennsylvania Reserves, Col. W. C. Talley; 2d Pennsylvania Reserves, Lieut.-Col. George A. Woodward; 6th Pennsylvania Reserves, Col. Wellington H. Ent; 11th Pennsylvania Reserves, Col. S. M. Jackson; 1st Rifles (Bucktails), Col. Charles J. Taylor.

Second Brigade—Col. Joseph W. Fisher, commanding; 5th Pennsylvania Reserves, Lieut-Col. George Dare; 9th Pennsylvania Reserves, Lieut-Col. James McK. Snodgrass; 10th Pennsylvania Reserves, Col. A. J. Warner; 12th Pennsylvania Reserves, Col. M. D. Hardin.

ARTILLERY BRIGADE.

Capt. A. P. Martin, commanding.

Battery D—5th United States, Lieut. Charles E. Hazlett.
Battery I—5th United States, Lieut. Leonard Martin.
Battery C—1st New York, Capt. Albert Barnes.
Battery L—1st Ohio, Captain N. C. Gibbs.

Battery E—Massachusetts, Captain A. P. Martin.
Provost Guard—Captain W. H. Ryder; Companies E and D, 12th New York.

SIXTH CORPS.

Major-General John Sedgwick.

FIRST DIVISION.

Brigadier-General H. G. Wright, commanding.
First Brigade—Brigadier-General A. T. A. Torbert; 1st New Jersey, Lieut-Col. William Henry, Jr.; 2d New Jersey, Col. Samuel L. Buck; 3d New Jersey, Col. Henry W. Brown; 15th New Jersey, Col. William H. Penrose.
Second Brigade—Brigadier-General J. J. Bartlett; 5th Maine, Col. Clarke S. Edwards; 121st New York, Col. Emory Upton; 95th Pennsylvania, Lieut-Col. Edward Carroll; 96th Pennsylvania, Lieut-Col. William H. Lessig.
Third Brigade—Brigadier-General D. A. Russell; 6th Maine, Col. Hiram Burnham; 49th Pennsylvania, Col. William H. Irvin, 119th Pennsylvania, Col. P. C. Ellmaker; 5th Wisconsin, Col. Thomas S. Allen.

SECOND DIVISION.

Brigadier-General A. P. Howe, commanding.
Second Brigade—Col. L. A. Grant, commanding; 2d Vermont, Col. J. H Walbridge; 3d Vermont, Col. T. O. Seaver; 4th Vermont, Col. E. H. Stoughton; 5th Vermont, Lieut-Col. John R. Lewis; 6th Vermont, Lieut-Col. Elisha L. Barney.
Third Brigade—Brigadier-General T. A. Neill; 7th Maine, Lieut-Col. Seldon Connor; 49th New York, Col. D. D. Bidwell; 77th New York, Col. J. B. McKean; 43d New York, Col. B. F. Baker; 61st Pennsylvania, Major George W. Dawson.

THIRD DIVISION.

Brigadier-General Frank Wheaton, commanding.
First Brigade—Brigadier-General Alexander Shaler; 65th New York, Col. J. E. Hamblin; 67th New York, Col. Nelson Cross; 122nd New York, Lieut-Col. A. W. Dwight; 23d Pennsylvania, Lieut-Col. J. F. Glenn; 82d Pennsylvania, Col. Isaac Bassett.
Second Brigade—Col. H. L. Eustis, commanding; 7th Massachusetts, Lieut-Col. Franklin P. Harlow; 10th Massachusetts, Lieut-Col. Jefford M. Decker; 37th Massachusetts, Col. Oliver Edwards; 2d Rhode Island, Col. Horatio Rogers.
Third Brigade—Col. David I. Nevin, 62d New York, commanding; 62d New York, Lieut-Col. Theodore P. Hamilton; 102 Pennsyl-

vania, Col. John W. Patterson ; 93d Pennsylvania, Col. James M. McCarter ; 98th Pennsylvania Major John B. Kohler ; 139th Pennsylvania, Lieut-Col. William H. Moody.

Artillery Brigade—Col. C. M. Tompkins, commanding ; Battery A, 1st Massachusetts, Capt. W. H. McCartney ; Battery D, 2d United States, Lieut. E. B. Williston ; Battery F, 5th United States, Lieut. Leonard Martin ; Battery G, 2d United States, Lieut. John H. Butler ; Battery C, 1st Rhode Island, Capt. Richard Waterman ; Battery G, 1st Rhode Island, Capt. George W. Adams ; 1st New York, Capt. Andrew Cowan ; 3d New York, Capt. William A. Harn.

Cavalry Detachment—Capt. William L. Craft, commanding ; Company H, 1st Pennsylvania ; Company L, 1st New Jersey.

ELEVENTH CORPS.

Major-General Oliver O. Howard, commander.

FIRST DIVISION.

Brigadier-General Francis C. Barlow, commanding.

First Brigade—Col. Leopold Von Gilsa, commanding ; 41st New York, Lieut-Col. D. Von Einsiedel ; 54th New York, Col. Eugene A. Kezley ; 68th New York, Col. Gotthilf Bourny de Ivernois ; 53d Pennsylvania, Col. Charles Glanz.

Second Brigade—Brigadier-General Adelbert Ames ; 17th Connecticut, Lieut-Col. Douglass Fowler ; 25th Ohio, Lieut-Col. Jeremiah Williams ; 75th Ohio, Col. A. L. Harris ; 107th Ohio, Captain John M. Lutz.

SECOND DIVISION.

Brigadier-General A. Von Steinwehr, commanding.

First Brigade—Col. Charles R. Coster, 134th New York, commanding ; 27th Pennsylvania, Lieut-Col. Lorenz. Cantador ; 73d Pennsylvania, Captain Daniel F. Kelley ; 134th New York, Lieut-Col. Allan H. Jackson ; 154th New York, Col. P. H. Jones.

Second Brigade—Col. Orlando Smith, commanding ; 33d Massachusetts, Lieut-Col. Adin B. Underwood ; 136th New York, Colone James Wood, Jr.; 55th Ohio, Col. Charles B. Gambee ; 73d Ohio, Lieut-Col. Richard Long.

THIRD DIVISION.

Major.General Carl Schurz, commanding.

First Brigade—Brigadier-General A. Von Schimmeepfennig, commanding ; 45th New York, Col. George Von Arnsburg ; 157th New York, Col. Philip P. Brown, Jr.; 74th Pennsylvania, Col. Adolph Von Hartung ; 61st Ohio, Col. S. J. McGroarty ; 82nd Illinois, Colonel J. Hecker.

Second Brigade—Col. Waldimer Kryzanowske, commanding; 58th New York, Lieut-Col. August Otto; 119th New York, Col. John T. Lockman; 75th Pennsylvania, Col. Francis Mahler; 82d Ohio, Col. James S. Robson; 26th Wisconsin, Col. William H. Jacobs.

Artillery Brigade—Major Thomas W. Osburn, commanding; Battery I, 1st New York, Capt. Michael Wiedrick; Battery I, 1st Ohio, Capt. Hubert Dilger; Battery K, 1st Ohio, Captain Lewis Heckman; Battery G, 4th United States, Lieut. Bayard Wilkeson; 13th New York, Lieut. William Wheeler.

TWELFTH CORPS.

Brigadier-General Alpheus S. Williams, commanding.

FIRST DIVISION.

Brigadier-General Thomas H. Ruger, commanding.

First Brigade—Col. Archibald L. McDougall; 5th Connecticut, Col. Warren W. Packer; 20th Connecticut, Lieut-Col. William B. Wooster; 123d New York, Col. A. L. McDougall; 145th New York, Col. E. L. Price; 46th Pennsylvania, Col. James L. Selfridge; 3d Maryland, Col. J. M. Sudsburg.

Second Brigade—Brigadier-General Henry H. Lockwood; 150th New York, Col. John H. Ketcham; 1st Maryland, (P. H. B.) Col. William P. Maulsby; 1st Maryland, (E. S.) Col. James Wallace.

Third Brigade—Col. Silas Calgrove, commanding; 2d Massachusetts, Col. Charles R. Mudge; 107th New York, Col. Miron M. Crane; 13th New Jersey, Col. Ezra A. Carman; 27th Indiana, Lieut-Col. John R. Fesler; 3d Wisconsin, Lieut-Col. Martin Flood.

SECOND DIVISION.

Brigadier-General John W. Geary, commanding.

First Brigade—Col. Charles Candy, 66th Ohio, commanding; 28th Pennsylvania, Captain John Flynn; 117th Pennsylvania, Lieut-Col. Ario Pardee, Jr.; 5th Ohio, Col. John H. Patrick; 7th Ohio, Col. William R. Creighton; 29th Ohio, Captain W. F. Stevens; 66th Ohio, Lieut-Col. Eugene Powell.

Second Brigade—1st Col. George A. Cobham, 2d Brig-Gen. Thomas L. Kane; 29th Pennsylvania, Col. William Rickards; 109th Pennsylvania, Capt. Frederick L. Gimber; 111th Pennsylvania, Lieut-Col. Thomas M. Walker.

Third Brigade—Brig-Gen. George S. Greene; 60th New York, Col. Abel'Godard; 78th New York, Lieut-Col. Herbert Von Hammerstein; 102d New York, Lieut-Col. James C. Lane; 137th New York, Col. David Ireland; 149th New York, Col. Henry A. Barnum.

ARTILLERY BRIGADE.

Lieut. E. D. Muhlenberg, commanding.
Battery F, 4th United States, Lieut. S. T. Rugg; Battery K, 5th United States, Lieut. D. H. Kinsie; Battery M, 1st New York, Lieut. Charles E. Winegar; Knapp's Pennsylvania Battery, Lieut. Charles Atwell.
Headquarter Guard—Battallion, 10th Maine.

CAVALRY CORPS.

Major-General Alfred Pleasanton, commanding.

FIRST DIVISION.

Brigadier-General John Buford, commanding.
First Brigade—Col. William Gamble, 8th Illinois, commanding; 8th New York, Col. Benjamin F. Davis; 8th Illinois, Lieut-Col. D. R. Clendenin; 2 squadrons, 12th Illinois, Col. Amoss Voss; 3 squadrons 3d Indiana, Col. George H. Chapman.
Second Brigade—Col. Thomas C. Devin, 6th New York, commanding; 6th New York, Lieut-Col. Wm. H. Crocker; 9th New York, Col. William Sackett; 17th Pennsylvania, Col, J. H. Kellogg; 3d Virginia, (detachment).
Reserve Brigade—Brig-Gen. Wesley Merritt; 1st United States, Captain R. S. C. Lord; 2d United States, Captain T. F. Rodenbough; 5th United States, Captain J. W. Mason; 6th United States, Major S. H. Starr, Captain G. C. Cram; 6th Pennsylvania, Major James H. Hazletine.

SECOND DIVISION.

Brig-General D. McM. Gregg, commanding.
(Headquarter Guard, Company A, 1st Ohio.)
First Brigade—Colonel J. B. McIntosh, commanding; 1st New Jersey, Major M. H. Beamont; 1st Pennsylvania, Col. John P. Taylor; 3d Pennsylvania, Lieut-Colonel Edward S. Jones; 1st Maryland, Lieut-Colonel James M. Deems; 1st Massachusetts, at Headquarters, 6th Corps.
Second Brigade—Colonel Pennock Huey, commanding; 2d New York, 4th New York, 8th Pennsylvania, 6th Ohio.

THIRD DIVISION.

Brigadier-General Judson Kilpatrick, commanding.
(Headquarter Guard, Company C, 1st Ohio.)
First Brigade—Brigadier-General E. J. Farnsworth; 5th New York, Major John Hammond; 18th Pennsylvania, Lieut-Col. William P. Brinton; 1st Vermont, Col. Edward D. Sawyer; 1st West Virginia, Colonel H. P. Richmond.

Second Brigade—Brigadier-General George A. Custer; 1st Michigan, Col. Charles H. Town ; 5th Michigan, Col. Russell A. Alger; 6th Michigan, Col. Greorge Gray ; 7th Michigan, Col. William D. Mann.

HORSE ARTILLERY.

First Brigade—Captain John M. Robertson, commanding ; Batteries B and L, 2d United States, Lieut. Edward Heaton ; Battery M, 2d United States, Lieut. A. C. M. Pennington ; Battery E, 4th United States, Lieut. S. S. Elder; 6th New York, Lieut. Joseph W. Martin ; 9th Michigan, Captain J. J. Daniels ; Battery C, 3d United States, Lieut. William D. Fuller.

Second Brigade—Captain John C. Tidball, commanding ; Batteries G and E, 1st United States, Capt. A. M. Randal ; Battery K, 1st United States, Capt. William M. Graham ; Battery A, 2d United States, Lieut. John Calef ; Battery C, 3d United States.

ARTILLERY RESERVE.

Brigadier-General R. O. Tyler.

First Regular Brigade—Capt. D. R. Ransom, commanding ; Battery H, 1st United States, Lieut. C. P. Eakin ; Batteries F and K, 3d United States, Lieut. J. C. Turnbull ; Battery C, 4th United States, Lieut. Evan Thomas ; Battery C, 5th United States, Lieut G. V. Weier.

First Voluntary Brigade—Lieut-Col. F. McGilvery, commanding, 15th New York, Capt. Patrick Hart ; Independent Battery Pennsylvania, Captain R. B. Ricketts ; 5th Massachusetts, Captain C. A. Phillips ; 9th Massachusetts, Captain John Bigelow.

Second Volunteer Brigade—Capt. E. D. Taft, commanding ; Batteries B and M, 1st Connecticut, 5th New York, Captain Elijah D. Taft ; 2d Connecticut, Lieut. John W. Sterling.

Third Volunteer Brigade—Capt. James F. Huntington, commanding ; Batteries F and G, 1st Pennsylvania, Capt. R. B. Ricketts ; Battery H, 1st Ohio, Capt. James F. Huntington ; Battery A, 1st New Hampshire, Capt. F. M. Edgell ; Battery C, 1st West Virginia, Capt. Wallace Hill.

Fourth Volunteer Brigade—Capt. R. H. Fitzhugh, commanding ; Battery B, 1st New York, Capt. James McRorty ; Battery G, 1st New York, Capt. Albert M. Ames ; Battery K, 1st New York, (11th Battery attached) Capt. R. H. Fitzhugh ; Battery A, 1st Maryland, Capt. James H. Rigby ; Battery A, 1st New Jersey, Lieut. Augustin N. Parsons ; 6th Maine, Lieut. Edwin B. Dow.

Train Guard—Major Charles Ewing, commanding ; 4th New Jersey Infantry.

Headquarter Guard—Capt. J. C. Fuller, commanding; Battery C, 32d Massachusetts.

Detachments at Headquarters, Army of the Potomac, during the battle of Gettysburg, under orders of the Provost Marshal General :—

Brigadier-General M. R. Patrick, commanding; 93d New York, 8th United States, 1st Massachusetts cavalry, 2d Pennsylvania cavalry, Batteries E and I, 6th Pennsylvania cavalry, Detachment regular cavalry; United States Engineer Battalion, Captain George H. Mendill, commanding.

Guards and Orderlies—Captain D. P. Mann, commanding; independent company Oneida cavalry.

Taking it for granted that the regiments averaged about the same number of men in each army, which we can reasonably do, perhaps the following lists will better enable the reader to comprehend the tremendous force brought to bear against each other in in that battle.

ARMY OF NORTHERN VIRGINIA.

States.	Infantry Reg'ts.	Cavalry.	Artillery.	Total.
Alabama,	13		2	15
South Carolina,	14	2	5	21
North Carolina,	36	4	4	44
Georgia,	38	3	7	48
Florida,	4			4
Louisiana,	10		7	17
Mississippi,	11		1	12
Virginia,	49	20	37	106
Maryland,	1	1	4	6
Arkansas,	1			1
Texas,	3			3
Tennessee,	3			3
	183	30	67	281

IN THE ARMY OF THE POTOMAC, AT GETTYSBURG:

States.	Infantry.	Cavalry.	Artillery.	Total.
Connecticut,	5		3	8
Delaware,	2			2
Illinois,	1	2		3
Indiana,	5	1		6
Maine,	10	1	3	14
Maryland,	3	2	1	6
Massachusetts,	19	2	4	25
Michigan,	7	4	1	12
Minnesota,	1			1
New Jersey,	12	1	2	15
New Hampshire,	3		1	4
New York,	69	8	15	92
Ohio,	13	1	4	18
Pennsylvania,	68	10	7	85
Rhode Island,	1		5	6
Vermont,	10	1		11
West Virginia,	1	2	1	4
Wisconsin,	6			6
U. S. Regulars,	13	4	25	42
	249	39	72	360

If nothing else can be found in my little book to recommend it, these, mostly official, and *all* as nearly accurate as can be gotten after twenty-five years, ought to give it a place in every house in the United States.

JO. M. KENDALL,

Lawyer,

Prestonsburg, - Kentucky.

☞ Practices especially in Floyd and adjoining counties, and in the higher State and Federal Courts.

☞ East Kentucky mineral and timber lands bought and sold. Correspondence solicited.

Walter S. Harkins,

ATTORNEY-AT-LAW,

Prestonsburg, Kentucky.

Will practice in the courts of Floyd, Johnson, Martin, Magoffin and Knott, and in the Superior and Appellate Courts of Kentucky.

☞ Has for sale 25,000 acres of Coal and Mineral Land, and 30,000 acres of Coal, Oil, Grass lands, &c.

References: Catlettsburg Nat. Bank, Catlettsburg, Ky.; John G. Johns, Esq., Prestonsburg, Ky.; Hon. W. C. Ireland, Ashland, Ky.; Hon. A. Dual, Frankfort, Ky.; Geo. W. McAlpin & Co., Cincinnati, O.; John F. Hager, Esq., Ashland, Ky.

CONNOLLY HOUSE,

Pikeville, Kentucky.

☞ New addition completed. All newly painted. Rooms neat, clean, and newly furnished. Charges reasonable. Good stable in connection. Daily hack line. The annex to the house, across the street, will soon be completed, which will give the house a capacity of 35 rooms,—good, &c.

The Proprietor is a Lawyer.

W. M. CONNOLLY, Prop'r.

WAYNE DAMRON,

WHOLESALE AND RETAIL DEALER IN

WHISKEY, WINE, BRANDY AND BEER.

Front Street, Catlettsburg, Ky.

Tom - and - Jerry - a - specialty.

Open from 4 A. M. until 10 P. M.

POOL AND BILLIARDS!

☞ Kentucky Hand-Made Sour-Mash Whiskey a specialty.

C. M. PARSONS.   J. M. ROBERSON.

PARSONS & ROBERSON,

ATTORNEYS-AT-LAW

AND REAL ESTATE AGENTS,

PIKEVILLE, PIKE COUNTY, KY.

Practice in the State and Federal Courts. Make a specialty of dealing in Mineral Lands in northeastern Kentucky.

☞ Abstracts of titles to lands in Pike county, furnished on short notice.

JAMES GOBLE,

ATTORNEY-AT-LAW

AND REAL ESTATE AGENT,

PRESTONSBURG, - - KY.

Practices in the Courts of eastern Kentucky, Superior Court and Court of Appeals, and U. S. Court.

Titles to real estate examined and abstracts made. Have some fine coal and timber land for sale.

C. CECIL, JR.,

—DEALER IN—

COOK & HEATING STOVES,

Glass and Queensware,

ROPE, BROOMS, &c.

Manufacturer and Jobber of TIN AND SHEET-IRON WARE.

No. 6 Front St., - - *CATLETTSBURG, KY.*

The Leading Wholesale and Retail Druggists.

CALVIN & PARSONS,

—KEEP CONSTANTLY ON HAND—

Drugs, Oils, Paints, Brushes of all kinds, Pocket Books, Toilet Soaps,

Notions, Perfumery, Toilet Articles, &c.

Sole Agents for Acker's, Gooch's and Chamberlain's Remedies, and all other standard Patent Medicines. Prescriptions carefully compounded.

☞ A fine line Cigars and Tobacco.
☞ Sole Proprietors for Rice's Anodyne Liniment.

NATIONAL HOUSE,

Next door to City Hall, near Main Street,

CHARLOTTESVILLE, - - VIRGINIA,

Mrs. Walter Brownley, Prop.

Best Location in the City. Good Accommodations.

☞ Rates, $1.00 and $1.25 per day.

PATTON BROS.,

ʰolesale Manufacturing Druggists,

CATLETTSBURG, - - KY.

The Largest Drug House in the Ohio Valley. Manufacturers of 228 Remedies that are sold by the Dozen. 16,000 square feet of floor room. 28 hands employed.

Sole Proprietors of the famous NERVE KING. The only remedy that is sold on an absolute guarantee to cure all Pains and Aches, Cramps and Colic, Diarrhœa, Dysentery, etc. Used internally and externally.

The best Liniment in the world. PRICE, 25 CENTS.

Sole Proprietors of the renowned HINDOO KIDNEY CORDIAL, for the permanent cure of Pains in the Back, and all disorders of the Kidneys and Urinary Organs.

Thousands of certificates of those who have used this remedy, will be sent on application. PRICE, $1.00.

☞ For sale by Drug Stores, and Country Stores everywhere. ☜

Gardner's Liniment

Is rapidly becoming known as an INFALLIBLE REMEDY for

Rheumatism, Neuralgia, Aches, Sprains, Bruises, Ingrowing Nails, Ulcers, Old Sores, Burns, Scalds, Toothache, &c., &c.

In a case of DIPHTHERIA take a feather with the liniment on it, after shaking well, and touch the infected parts and you will get relief.

Try it on a SORE-BACK HORSE, or any of the aforesaid troubles in horses or cattle, and note the effect. It will always help and often cure them.

I know that when it is once tried in a city, town, or country, a demand is secured for it.

Druggists, merchants, and dealers generally, this remedy must reach the people, and the sooner you take hold of it the better—not only for you, but for me, for suffering humanity, and many of the brute creation.

Call on the merchants for it, and if they will not get it for you send to me, and when you get it always keep it in the house for unforeseen emergencies, and strictly observe the directions on the bottle.

In all the multifarious diseases that this remedy will eradicate or help, it is essential that the bowels be kept in a healthy condition.

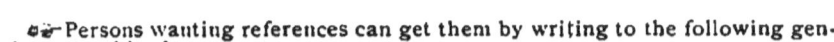

☞ Persons wanting references can get them by writing to the following gentlemen at this place :

W. H. SOWARDS, Postmaster; REV. JESSE BALL; REV. GEO. STUMP; REV. C. N. JOHNSON; HARRY WEDDINGTON, Deputy Sheriff; HI WILLIAMSON, Clerk Pike County Court; F. C. HATCHER, Vice-President Pike County Farmers' and Laborers' Union; A. J. AUXIER, Attorney-at-Law; Ex-U. S. Marshal of Kentucky.

PRICE 25 CENTS.
C. R. GARDNER, Pikeville, Ky.

BIG SANDY
HACK LINE CO.

RUNS DAILY HACKS

(Except Sundays) between Richardson, Paintsville, Prestonsburg and Pikeville, Ky.

THE ONLY RELIABLE LINE

running daily from the railroad to Pikeville.

Good Feed and Livery Stables.

where conveyances can be hired for any part of county, both at Paintsville and Prestonsburg. Special attention given to forwarding

BAGGAGE AND EXPRESS.

For any information desired, address

Big Sandy Hack Line,

Paintsville or Prestonsburg, Ky

JOHN B. SANFORD,

CATLETTSBURG, KY.,

Manufacturer of and dealer in all kinds of

SADDLES, HARNESS, BRIDLES, COLLARS, WHIPS, Etc.

☞ The famous KENTUCKY SPRING SADDLE a specialty.

For a number of years Mr. Sanford has devoted his entire time to the manufacture of this excellent SADDLE, and the truth of the superiority of this saddle over all other saddles, is manifested to him by the orders he receives for it from all parts of the country, many of them being shipped to remote sections.

The points of superiority of this saddle consist in its being built in such a manner as to adapt itself both to the horse and to the rider, so as not to hurt either; and any person who has any regard for self or horse, having once tried this saddle, will never use any ⁀er; and purchasers are numerous who
re they would not take ten prices
ere it impossible to obtain an-
ᵣr. Sanford not only supplies
ʰroughout his own section of
₁ them, but ships them to
₁tucky, West Virginia, Ohio,
them to nearly every State

ps a full line of SADDLES
ARNESS OF EVERY KIND,
ything connected with the Sad-
Harness business.

ᵓLES SENT TO ANY STATE
CT TO EXAMINATION.

☞ Correspondence solicited. Mail orders
mptly filled.

www.ingramcontent.com/pod-product-compliance
Lightning Source LLC
Chambersburg PA
CBHW030435190426
43202CB00036B/1315